Santayana, Art, and Aesthetics

A Case Institute of Technology Book
in the Humanities and Social Sciences

Santayana, Art, and Aesthetics

JEROME ASHMORE

■

The Press of Western Reserve University : 1966

■

To F with love

Preface

Santayana's theories of art and aesthetics have been treated previously in two excellent books: Irving Singer's *Santayana's Aesthetics* and W. E. Arnett's *Santayana and the Sense of Beauty*. What is the warrant, then, for another book about the same sector of Santayana's thought? Only the ordinary point that there are aspects of this sector worthy of attention and not emphasized in the two extant books. As usual, there is another way to approach the same subject matter.

Mr. Singer and Mr. Arnett each assume a different perspective. Mr. Singer is concerned mainly with adverse criticism of Santayana's position in aesthetics and with comparisons of this position with one projected by Mr. Singer himself on the basis of emendations of Santayana's doctrines. Again, when Mr. Singer brings forward questions relevant to the constitution of human experience, to epistemology, and to value theory, he places Santayana's corresponding views on trial by comparison with those of John Dewey and C. I. Lewis and suggests remedial measures. He also affirms the general belief that the distinction between essence and existence is a cardinal element in Santayana's entire philosophy and from this premise infers that this distinction is primary in Santayana's aesthetics and philosophy of art. But Mr. Singer tends to consider the essence-existence relation as deployed in epistemology rather than in ontology and also to turn to pragmatism as a guide to resolution of nonpragmatic issues.

For the most part Mr. Singer approaches Santayana's aesthetics by proposing dichotomies resembling those found in Santayana and then offering original resolutions of these dichotomies. Yet in so doing he is holding to his avowed objective of forming an aesthetic theory of his own based on that of Santayana. It turns out, then, that Mr. Singer's work is, in large part, an exhibition of his own theoretical suggestions; but when he does refer to some of the fundamentals in Santayana's aesthetics his treatment is lucid, is helpful, and, although compressed, is comprehensive.

Mr. Arnett is concerned mainly with the aesthetic quality suggested by all of Santayana's theories, in other words with the aura of beauty and the aesthetic affinities and preoccupations that were manifest no matter what field occupied Santayana's mind. Mr. Arnett's work depicts Santayana as representing an aesthetic temperament communing with essence. From such a perspective it is odd that the emphasis in the development of Mr. Arnett's theme is not in ontology but in human experience. He sees Santayana's aesthetic temperament as something derived from intuition and from the fact that intuition generates aesthetic character by being more concerned with form and with possibility than with other aspects of what is apprehended. He supports his conviction by pointing to Santayana's moral philosophy and ontology, where form and potentiality are crucial factors. Of course, Santayana definitely considered contemplative experience, expecially of essences, as aesthetic and also definitely stood for rational ideals as a formal projection. Mr. Arnett proposes that a resultant of a combination of these two directions will be the conclusion that "it is poetry, religion, and all the fine arts that serve the spirit best, not by indicating what the world is, but by their suggestions of what the world might be"[1] and that thereby a moral ideal becomes something aesthetic. A corollary will be that in Santayana's philosophy aesthetic qualities are integral parts of whatever is worth having or doing and that it is the form of things, not their movement, that is the justification of the good life.[2] Also "that action acquires worth only in proportion to the delight found in either the object created or in the consummation reached in the activity itself, (or both)"[3] and that the aesthetic appeal of an idea plays a major role in determining what philosophy an individual will accept. It will follow that beauty is more fundamental to human happiness than truth.

The present essay is expository to a greater extent than it is critical and is offered as a study and a commentary rather than as a piece of creative interpretation. It is quite distinct from the essay of Mr. Singer for it is not a piece of sustained criticism nor is it a medium for propounding a new aesthetic theory. It is not so sharply separated from Mr. Arnett's work, the difference being mainly in aspects selected for emphasis. Mr. Arnett directs his attention to the aesthetic category as an agent unifying Santayana's philosophy and to the functional aspects of this category in respect to human experience. Although Santayana's aesthetic theory unquestionably is interpolated with his moral philosophy and carries a moral burden, the present work slights the moral consequences that Mr. Arnett, following Santayana, constantly has in mind. Instead it chooses to look not at a wishful prospect of man's progress, his practice of various arts and consequent realization of happiness, but at the raw elements in the structure and foundations of Santayana's aesthetic theory. That is, the essay gives more attention to the primitive parts in the genesis and organization of Santayana's aesthetic theory than to the apotheosis of them. It proceeds with a historical accent, aiming to see the details of Santayana's contribution to the field of aesthetics and to what extent this contribution pertains to fine art. If the essay has a thesis, it is that fine art does not occupy a central position in Santayana's aesthetics, that his aesthetic theory is closely associated with psychology, with essences, and with moral goals but not with fine art.

The above comments do not imply that any of the three essays mentioned excludes the other two as an aid to the study of Santayana's aesthetics. Rather it is presumed that each supplements the others and that together they offer a broader understanding of the topic than any one of them would by itself.

The courtesy of Mr. Norman Malcolm and of the following publishers and periodicals in permitting the use of copyrighted material is acknowledged gratefully: *The American Scholar*, George Braziller, Inc., Charles Scribner's Sons, Harvard University Press, Holt, Rinehart and Winston, Inc., Indiana University Press, J. M. Dent and Sons, Ltd., The Open Court Publishing Company, Philosophical Library, *Saturday Review*, and the University of Pennsylvania Press.

Thanks also are extended to Case Institute of Technology for providing the opportunity to complete the manuscript, and in particular to D. Harvey Buchanan, John Pierce, and David Rein of the Case Department of Humanities and Social Studies for countless expressions of good will and encouragement. There are many others whose reassurance has been most helpful. Howard Webber's guidance among the ways of the publishing field and the expert secretarial assistance of Joan Copeland and Susan Gallop are recognized and greatly appreciated. However none of the above individuals is responsible for whatever inadequacies may be present in the book.

JEROME ASHMORE
Cleveland, Ohio

Contents

Santayana, Art, and Aesthetics

CHAPTER I

Introduction

∎

To all who would judge that Santayana had developed theories of art and aesthetics of his own, he issues warning that he has not.[1] But the interpretation of this injunction need not be categorical. An examination of Santayana's writings reveals the qualification that he never held an art theory or wrote an aesthetics considered as something entirely distinctive and dissociated from a larger and enveloping theory of rational living, happiness, and freedom. Insofar as theories of art and aesthetics may be separated from moral philosophy, Santayana utterly rejects them;[2] but insofar as they are an indispensable part of it, he embraces them warmly.[3] Within a theory of morals Santayana includes theories of art[4] and aesthetics[5] that obviously are products of keen sensitivity and a vast store of knowledge.

For Santayana there is no unique and independent aesthetic experience associated with fine art,[6] nor may fine or other art be separated from the sphere of morals[7] to possess some sort of self-containment. His sense of rational harmony is offended by any kind of segregation that assumes isolated theory and isolated functioning of elements segregated.[8] A separate theory of art in general, if it led to anything, would lead to works with no subject or meaning or moral glow;[9] while "to abstract a so-called aesthetic interest from all other interests . . . is to make the aesthetic sphere contemptible."[10] In a larger sense, Santayana is affirming that there is mutual

1

interdependence among values, the end of which is to maintain the integrity of each. The harmonious integration of values in reason requires that the value, beauty, be included within it; in like manner the harmonious integration of all moral action requires the inclusion of art. In both cases failure to integrate entails loss of significance.

There is, then, a certain indispensable unity that Santayana postulates among aesthetic value, moral value, and the rational activity that is art. But, though empirically inseparable, Santayana's theories of art and aesthetics are logically distinguishable, and with the objective of tentative examination the study of each may be conducted separately. In a way there is clarification by looking at the two theories individually, for they have different bearing: the aesthetics is concerned with beauty as a value and with the psyche and its psychology; the theory of art rises from aboriginal human existence as the source of techniques that have evolved to instrumentalities crucial to rational programs for happiness. There is, within the large comprehension of what is moral in Santayana's view, a body of knowledge descriptive of aesthetics and another descriptive of art, and the present study seeks to reveal the components and presuppositions of each. Santayana proclaimed a linkage of the two and an absorption of both by morals, and it is through no design of his that to some they may appear more lucid if separated. Since he never was a doctrinaire but was instead a genuine artist, his work admits of more than one interpretation.[11]

Santayana's technical achievement in aesthetics and art theory intentionally is not of large proportions, yet he throws upon both fields a great amount of illumination. He avoids argumentation and explicit direct answers to hypothetical objections, although there is an undercurrent in his writing that indirectly amounts to a skillful defense of the trend of his thought. Anyone attempting to demolish his position will encounter considerable unexpected resistance. His statements progress in a distinctive way and usually are unified by a characteristic emotional tone, but their color and warmth often disguise a systematic exposition that seems to result from an unconscious ordering within Santayana's mind rather than from a preconceived arrangement of presentation. He frequently resorts to an enchanting metaphor that he is quite willing to let serve as an explanation of a persuasion. He commonly writes with the attitude of a spectator, yet his observations resemble musings, memoirs, or a soliloquy. But above all his native genius produces an abundance of valuable insights any time he decides to turn his thoughts to beauty[12] or to morals.

Santayana has one of the truly profound modern minds, distinguished by its rapport with objects evoking beauty. But it is a mind harboring inexpugnable contraries. For example, Santayana's aesthetics, in one aspect, is essentially romantic: the individual determines and interprets value; in another aspect it is essentially classic: there is a rational order that is a moral goal, and correlation with this order determines the place of any other value. The value that has its source in limited natural and individual impulse, and is therefore relative and biased, is not in itself decisive as to its own status but depends on reason, which while not itself a value is a supreme standard for the functioning of value. These two poles, ideal and natural, have both hereditary and environmental antecedents. Santayana's mind by heredity was a product of an art-loving father with a studious nature and an austere mother who lived by sets of rigid morals that strangely were based on a semi-revolutionary social outlook, which included the belief that people were made good not by religion but by reason. His mind environmentally was exposed to the contrasting forces represented by stable, tranquil Avila, a cathedral city of Catholic Spain, and changing, busy Boston, a stronghold of New England Puritanism; by Royce's idealism and James's empiricism; by Lotze's aesthetic metaphysics and Ebbinghaus' physiological psychology. Other influences were the doctrines of Georg Simmel and Friedrich Paulsen. Simmel looked to the physical base of impulse and habit for the origin of abstract conceptions and further appealed to Santayana by his opposition to formalism as in Kant and his affirmation of life as in Goethe, while Paulsen's presentation of Greek rational ethics was an especially decisive influence. All of these antecedents left marks discernible in Santayana's work and to that extent contributed to the tone of contrariety emanating from his thought. Brand Blanshard notes that even Santayana's famed materialism is not forthrightly corporeal after the manner of Hobbes and Democritus but is equivocally a naturalistic ideal after the manner of Aristotle.[13]

In examining Santayana's writings having a relevance to aesthetics, we cannot assume that he intends to assert a comprehensive unified system. He will not take the responsibility of either composing an aesthetics or of presenting one to us.[14] His work has to point to an aesthetic theory rather than expound one. In such a light, the foundation of Santayana's aesthetics and art theory will be a concatenation of the self, morals, reason, and happiness. In the stream of thought that yields these theories the main current concerns a moral order which is not only the objective and the goal of our living but is at the same time an ultimate structure pervading our immediate environment as well as the rest of the universe. Although this moral envelope cannot be perceived by the senses, it can be reached by activities starting within the senses, and moreover, it has a definite relation to the functioning of the senses. We find within it three essential principles that are major influences in man's aesthetic experiences and production of art.

The first is the subjective self regarded as a unit of psychic and physiological behavior and the raw material for values, for conformity with reason, and for happiness. It is basically empirical in character and the aesthetic dimension as found within it is relative and individualistic. The self is a receptacle for vital impulses that subsequently become transfigured within a rational structure envisaged and sought by man, and the outcome of the process will be the kind of compensation in living that is known as happiness.

The second principle is the rational ordering which brings diversity into unity and proportion. According to Santayana the harmonizing of diverse interests within the self is a function which represents reason.[15] When the activities of the self follow the formal harmony designated as reason, the consequence is a state of happiness and an approach to perfection. For Santayana, then, aesthetics is one segment both of a rational life and of a happy existence; and art is the activity by which the rational life and happiness are approached. The sense in which he uses the term "reason" differs from the usual connotation found in mathematics, law, or science. Santayana does not identify reason with any of these. Instead reason is something almost self contained, with its character traceable to its properties of harmony, sanity, and integration. A distinguishing mark of Santayana's reason is that it is not mediate or discursive; it is its own object of thought. Yet it is a practical goal and offers the reward of happiness and perfect living. Reason is at the same time itself and the object of human experience.[16] The harmony between the individual's impulses and activities toward his environment is at once a happy state and an exemplification of reason.

The third principle guiding aesthetic experience, and assumed by the rational ideal, is one of happiness or perfection in living.

Happiness is a consequence of reason, just as reason is the consequence of harmonious merging of individual interests. Happiness becomes the end or summation of man's individual experience and closes a circle in which each component arc reinforces the other: human experience, reason, and human happiness mutually interact in a total situation.[17] All three components of perfect living are available to man and to all men. But the presence of desires emphasizes the point that the situation concerns first of all man as the individual. For Santayana the interests of the collection of individuals comprising a social group reduce to fundamentally separated individual interests.[18] It is the single human organism that is the point of contact with value, with reason, and with happiness.

Santayana's reason, which is the key and control of his art theory, is neither a psychological state or process nor a discursive ordering. It seems to be something like an immaterial structure or matrix available to the interests of man and correlative to them as well.[19] Reason implies a result of activity on the part of the human individual or at least the structural goal toward which human behavior tends when it is positively aesthetic and when it is moral;[20] and when it is positively aesthetic it is also moral.[21] In a way, approved individual behavior is both a tendency *toward* reason and a kind of conduct *according to* reason. In turn, reason has a twofold character, being both the form of the plan for balanced human behavior of the individual and the behavior identifying itself with this form. Human behavior exemplifies reason by organization with respect to itself, with respect to natural environment, and with respect to the art products which result from interaction with the environment. By conciliating all claims of the self's varied impulses, the individual attains reason.[22] Reason is not exhaustively analyzable into properties but reveals some that may be construed as order or harmony and as equilibrium or sanity.[23] It is not a given external standard for the self to simulate, but instead is grounded in the behavior of the self, and is variable *according to individuals*. It does not pre-exist but acquires existence when a set of conditions are fulfilled.[24] To some extent the human self creates reason. It seems as if Santayana regarded pure reason as a kind of colorless entelechy that could become realized by acquiring human content.[25] Reason, however, is not of the character of something a priori.[26] The a priori, although having unqualified authority, especially in cognitive operations, is removed from life, is ineffable, and is ethically neutral; reason is something partaking of life, synonymous of the good, and productive of happiness. Reason is a state of structure and function that makes perfection out of imperfection; the rational principle takes from the self imperfect parts and gives them form that creates the medium for a perfection of life.

In treating art and aesthetics Santayana obtains a unity of views in a concrete, personal way that has no concern with whether or not the result coheres with excluded conditions in a way that would produce a universal system. That is, he is not seeking something architectonic. He avoids what he would consider an icy system of abstractions[27] and prefers to see mind and body as parts and products of nature with thoughts and feelings that are continuous with the natural order and not a separate formulation of it.

Although Santayana offers no isolated theory of art or aesthetics, he devoted three complete books,[28] a large part of two others,[29] and numerous articles to a presentation of his sentiments in these fields. Moreover, in their moral dimension, aesthetics was for him a major part of experience and art a major part of living. It is likewise apparent that the character of his views of art and aesthetics influenced his discussions of other topics. The chief aim of this essay is to detect what is presupposed and what is affirmed in this selected area of Santayana's thought, and to subject the result to examination within an exposition intended to be constructive. The restrictions of this objective exclude questions of contemplation of "essences" as spiritual experience with an aesthetic character, and the metaphysical context of such questions, as presented by Santayana in *Realms of Being* and other later works.[30]

The study begins with a consideration of what Santayana saw happen when a self is presented with products of art, nature, or machines; it continues with an examination of how he viewed criticism and poetry, then proceeds to his theory of art, and finally touches on some of his comments classed as supplementary to what he has asserted previously. The continuity of this mode of approach corresponds to the chronological order in which Santayana presented his aesthetics and art theory. The order is not strictly an evolutionary development, however, since all of the phases were partially explicit in Santayana's thinking before each was given separate emphasis, and the distinction made among them for convenience in investigation must not be allowed to interfere with the original conceptual unity from which each emerges.

CHAPTER II

Aesthetic Experience

∎

1. *The Psychological Foundation of Beauty as a Value*

In *The Sense of Beauty*, which Santayana characterizes as an outline of his aesthetic theory,[1] he presents a clear exposition of the subjective self[2] as a vehicle of aesthetic dynamics. In this work he accepts as foundational assumptions both hedonism and mechanism. Pleasure is good and pain is bad; while one of the chief objectives in mapping the field of aesthetics is to distinguish aesthetic pleasures from other kinds. In the steps toward this delimitation Santayana relies on some assumptions consistent with a mechanistic naturalism. First, he assumes feelings are derived entirely from the physiology of the human organism and therefore that feeling has a spatio-temporal location and a physico-chemical base responsive to laws of physical bodies; and second, that because of such subjective origin, one man's feelings do not duplicate another's.

Santayana reaches the sphere of aesthetic behavior by a series of exclusions from an original large and general domain: the entire universe seen under mutually exclusive categories of mechanism and consciousness. When the universe is considered as entirely physical, it is *ipso facto* entirely mechanical and will have no consciousness.[3] But, by being devoid of consciousness, the physical world is devoid also of value, for in Santayana's postulation value occurs only within consciousness.[4] However, within consciousness itself there is a portion that will contain value and one that will not; in the portion of consciousness denoted as intellectual, value cannot be located. Santayana says of this intellectual content that in it "every event would . . . be noted, its relations would be observed, its recurrence might even be expected; but all this would happen without a shadow of desire, of pleasure, or of regret. . . . We might have a world of idea without a world of will."[5] The intellectual processes of consciousness must be decanted and that step will leave a residue of feeling that is inseparable from vital impulses and is likewise the home of values.[6]

But even with the location of values isolated, the aesthetic values cannot become objects for examination until they are discriminated from moral values. This required discrimination is accomplished by limiting moral values to the characteristics of negation[7] and instrumentality,[8] leaving a remainder of pure aesthetic value.

The aesthetic value thus obtained is recognized as intrinsic and equated with pleasure, encountering then the need to discriminate those pleasures which are perceptions of beauty from those which are not.[9] For the purpose of this discrimination pleasures that are not perceptions of beauty are denoted as bodily or physical pleasures and distinguished from aesthetic pleasure by being those "that call to our attention some part of our own body, and which make no object so conspicuous to us as the organ in which they arise";[10] in aesthetic pleasure the organs "must be transparent, they must not intercept our attention, but carry it directly to some external object."[11] But even at this stage in the analysis, precautions must be taken to identify the criterion of genuine aesthetic pleasure and avoid misleading substitutes found in the characteristics of universality and disinterestedness. It is neither universality nor disinterestedness that determines aesthetic value. To become a truly aesthetic value and to qualify for further explication, a pleasure must partake of the act of "objectification" which is "the transformation of an element of sensation into the quality of a thing." The plane for the study of aesthetics will be the plane of objectified pleasure.

This act of "objectification" involving pleasure is analogous to the process that we apply to colors when we apparently see them as qualities on the surfaces of the external objects. But colors, like all other sensations, are correlated with human physiological activities. When, therefore, colors are perceived as if they were qualities on the surfaces of external objects, such pseudo-location is established by a psychological process of projection. Santayana is affirming a doctrine that both emotions and impressions of sense are capable of objectification.[12]

In the case of colors, shapes, and other images taken to be qualities of the object, the interrelationships in perception remain comparatively constant, making this kind of data easy to objectify by past habitual experience. In contrast, pleasures and pains are variable in their association with objects and tend to be associated with the organism[13] and therefore, one might say, to be subjectified. However, when this common tendency is reversed and a pleasure is objectified, it appears to be incorporated in an external object along with the colors and textures of the object. Under such conditions aesthetic perception occurs and the value, beauty, originates.[14] The process takes place without a division of perception whereby the subject contributes to part of what is happening and the object to the rest.[15] The aesthetic experience itself, not the object or the consequences of the experience, is what matters.

In Santayana's analysis the elements of our nature which make us sensible of beauty and the constitution of the real object toward which our experience of beauty is directed are exclusive of each other. The real object is definitely not a container of beauty and beauty is definitely not something noumenally objective. The experiencing organism is the source of beauty and aesthetics concerns itself with the perception of values. Emphatically the external thing toward which the self's impulses react does not share the value character of the reaction.[16] Yet it cannot be concluded that Santayana implies the external object is "nothing" or that he believes it insignificant in the aesthetic sensing.[17] What he contends is that the external thing of nature or art or other order is quite different from the subject's appreciation of it as beautiful, which being a value does not have the constitution of a thing. The value experience cannot be contained in the external object, simply because the value experience arises from the self's vital impulses. As a consequence the real external object always occupies a secondary place in Santayana's aesthetics.

The value, beauty, is neither a real nor a phenomenal object of human desire. On the contrary, beauty, in its primitive state, is identical with desire. Beauty is no more than human desire pleased by satisfying itself in outer reference.[18] Merely within the normal processes of consciousness beauty transcends its dark embryonic location in the conative complex of the human organism to become pleasure and a value. In other words, within the irrational depths of the organism Santayana postulates a governing agent, which in some way must be the author or basis of all beauty. That this prime agent cannot be cognitive is clear.[19] To include the form and process of thought would involve some kind of correspondence, identity, or other relation between the thinker and some real or phenomenal object with the likelihood of a control over the thought by either kind of object. But Santayana will not allow any object to participate in the determination of a value the way it might in the determination of a thought. For him the character of a value is never determined as a property resident in an independent object.[20] The cognitive realm is distinct from the realm of value[21] and cannot be more than auxiliary among factors leading to pleasure.

Frequently, in schematization of psychological factors, sense perception is associated with the faculty of intelligence and pleasure with the passions. Santayana revises this orthodoxy in the case of aesthetic experience. Aesthetically sense perception is connected with pleasure and intelligence is of service to the passions.[22] However he by no means urges a view that there are living cleavages in human consciousness. The experiencing self is unquestionably one unbroken process. Terminology such as perception, pleasure, passion, and intelligence is for Santayana only a logical device employed for convenience in examining the constituents of the category labelled consciousness. Abstractly considered, a perception-pleasure relation may be seen as a condition for the value experience and that is the chief point Santayana wishes to make in this context. Stated in broader terms, Santayana will maintain that activity of a physiological mechanism is required before a psychic sublimation can occur. The ultimately objectified pleasure which is beauty is a distinctive sort of entity. It is something divorced from thought in the sense that the existence of beauty never depended on thought; it is also transcendent with respect to impulse and instinct because even though they are the locus of its origin, a series of transformations within processes of consciousness leaves beauty at a stage that bears little resemblance to this origin.[23]

In Santayana's outlook values are individualistically human,[24] not superimposed by the authority of any well-informed person or of any arbitrary scale. When we affirm value is human, we deny one value cutting across many selves, just as we would deny there is one toothache that everyone should seek and experience. From the premise that there is a multiplicity of human feeling, it follows that there is a multiplicity of sensing and of valuing. This multiplicity does not require any unity transcending it; for Santayana there is neither a principle nor an ideal of beauty. Beauty is relative and pluralistic and otherwise does not exist.[25] Not even agreement by many individuals as to the beauty correlated with some object would be warrant for establishing that object as a standard of beauty or for using the agreement as a basis for formulating some law of beauty.[26] If there are laws of beauty they are in physiological psychology, not in objects. Beauty has nothing to do with either aggregates or standards whether formed by counting or by insight. Any common factor within some alleged totality of beauty would neglect much of the quality of individual cases used in the speculation. That kind of common factor and presumed totality is ignored by Santayana.

According to Santayana, the value, beauty, occurs pluralistically on a psycho-physical basis. From this plurality of beauty there is no intellectual or other operation that will lead to an induction of a unity. Nor will any eternal form or divine being be sufficient as a pattern for beauty or be a participant in it. Santayana's aesthetics is atomistic and will not adapt itself either to generalization or to idealistic metaphysics. We have to approach beauty through relative, individual pleasure. The pleasure reaches toward an outside object in conjunction with the apprehension of this object by sense; and thereby pleasure grasps a matrix for the objectification of itself. But the value of the pleasure starts in a vital impulse, not in the outside object. What must this impulse be? We do not know for it is irrational; we merely admit valuation rests on an irrational premise. Human desire stirs in compresence with a mysterious agitating agent. Thereupon desire finds itself poised to project something outside of itself to a focal point that might be called an object *for* beauty. The psychic state is necessarily one of pleasure, and the pleasure has to be related to the sensing of the focal object, presumably so that the pleasure may be definitely experienced instead of aborted in diffusion. In becoming the value which is beauty, pleasure seeks something external by means of which it may objectify itself, some kind of stable, but inscrutable, ground on which it may light. Yet it distinguishes itself in this objectification. The resource for the valuation is the impulse and the pleasure; the experience of the valuation comes to be with the assistance of the focal object.

2. *Value from Materials*

After identifying beauty as "pleasure regarded as the quality of a thing,"[27] Santayana explains how the senses contribute to the pleasure that is transformed into beauty. The transformation wherein the organism's apprehension becomes beauty occurs under three aspects, these being of material, of form, and of expression.

The fundamental materials of beauty are human functions.[28] For Santayana it is not some outer substance which is the material of beauty, it is the psychic and physiological action of the organism. It is by virtue of physiological and psychic acts that man is able to achieve the pleasure that goes outward as beauty.[29] Although the senses of sight and hearing are the principal elements specifically entering into the psychological creation of beauty, there are other sources of a more organically diffuse character that nevertheless influence the total accomplishment. Among these Santayana mentions love as a passion and social instincts.

The passion of love natively is accommodated to the instinctive and physiologically mechanistic reactions of sex which, unlike some of the other instincts, does not tend to become unconscious. Rather, it emits radiations that clothe the contemplation of certain things of the outer world with a warmth congenial to beauty.[30] However, the passion of love and instinct of sex are still secondary factors with respect to beauty, since they do not react within the situation until the senses have indicated the object of the organism's pleasure.[31] That is to say, the given stimulus to sexual passion must have beforehand its own aesthetic merit, which the sexual passion will augment[32] but does not originate.[33] More indirect than the influence of the passion of love is that of social instincts.[34] Social objects and their accompaniments, such as friendship, wealth, and reputation, are hampered in contributing to aesthetic experience because of lack of adaptation to definite imagery;[35] while these may be objects of desire, they are, as psychological materials, abstract and verbal rather than sensuous. They are not experienced in sensory immediacy as qualities of some physical object, and therefore the pleasure derived from them is obstructed from objectification.

Basically and for the most part, the materials of beauty are developed from the eye and the ear. The organs of perception give us the materials out of which we construct objects to which we attach beauty. By reason of its own given operations, the human organism is a beauty-making machine. Placed in contact with a colorless, odorless, tasteless, textureless, silent, mysterious, resistant outer domain, it manufactures phenomenal objects,[36] pleasure,[37] and aesthetic values.[38] Each of the five senses participating in this processing has the aptitude to contribute to beauty.[39] It is the senses that fill in the non-sensuous outer world with the multitude of qualities we say this world has. Yet even with all the attributions to the world by consciousness, there may arise a situation in which the organism may lack a response of charm or delight and thereby be denied an aesthetic tone. It is quite conceivable that we should have experience of outer objects as predominantly observational and intellectual with the apprehension void of desire, pleasure, pain, or regret, that is to say, that we should experience a world without values, the kind of world science constantly seeks to construct. But for Santayana, if the apprehended world is to be "any good," emotion must enter it. Appreciation of the phenomenal objects is required: mere consciousness of them will not suffice, emotional consciousness of them must occur.[40] With the advent of emotion within consciousness and the tingeing of experience with pleasure which may be objectified to generate beauty, the materials of consciousness become aesthetic and the senses acquire a new importance.

Pleasures of sensation are elemental to beauty and it is abstracted sensations that make the beauty of the materials of things.[41] There is, on Santayana's part, a strong identification of sensuousness with beauty. And, after the manner of the Greeks, he proclaims sight and hearing as the aesthetic senses in differentiation from taste, smell, and touch which he designates as non-aesthetic. His criterion for the differentiation is quite definite. Sight and hearing have the rank of aesthetic senses because they afford physically measurable[42] phenomenal objects having structure and an identifiable location; the remaining senses do not. Therefore sight and hearing[43] are readily adaptable to the objectifying activity of the understanding; the remaining senses are not.[44] The relation between the aesthetic and non-aesthetic or lower senses is not one of exclusion[45] but of relative importance in consummating the value of beauty. Sight and hearing dominate in this accomplishment; the other senses are subordinate.

"Sensuous beauty," Santayana remarks, "is not the greatest or most important element of effect, but it is the most primitive, and the most universal."[46] The outstanding characteristic of sensuous beauty is a pervasiveness whereby in itself it commands its own sphere of value, and at the same time it is a kind of ground[47] that augments and enlivens effects of beauty from other correlates, especially effects considered formal.[48]

3. *Value from Form*

After accounting for the nature of beauty and examining the role of the material factor or sensuous surface in the occurrence of beauty, Santayana turns to another consideration found in effects which are not traceable to sensuous surface but rather to certain ideal relations that accompany the object presented for apprehension. These relations, while they transcend the effect of the sensuous surface, or as Prall called it, aesthetic surface, are enhanced by that effect, not segregated from it;[49] in fact, they are an actual arrangement of it.[50] The resulting advance in degree of beauty is contingent on the factor of form, which for Santayana is fundamental to questions in the field of aesthetics.[51]

The acknowledgment of such a fact as beauty of form raises questions concerning what phase of the aesthetic experiential process contains this kind of beauty and what the relation of this phase to other phases of the same process may be. Santayana answers these questions by locating beauty of form between two poles, one the simple delight in sensuous surface, the other a field entirely excluding the senses — that of attention to ideas associated with the object, ignoring the idea of the object itself. Within the intermediate zone and independent of, in the sense of not being a consequence of, either pole lie a collection of sensible units, which if singly considered are indifferent with respect to activating the sense of beauty but in combination please the subject and allow the value which is beauty to be projected.[52] Pleasure as active in beauty of form must be treated as distinct from each of the encompassing poles: from delight in the sensuous surface and from other pleasure in the associated idea.[53]

The province of form, then, is the combination of discretely indifferent elements that pleases. Furthermore form is coexistent with some material,[54] even though aesthetically distinguishable from this material. Form and material are correlative in existence and separable in effect, yet material is capable of enhancing form.[55] Santayana omits consideration of the question of whether form enhances material, but comes close to denying this possibility by referring to form as originating a higher beauty with material as the groundwork for it.[56]

How does beauty from form occur? Santayana begins the answer to this question by referring to some physiology of perception. He notes that in the case of visual perception there is a point-for-point representation of the object's form observable on the retina and adds the remark that a similar construction of an image is not to be found in the functioning of other sense organs.[57] Yet with due caution he does not assume that the relative position of elements in the image on the retina is transmitted to the brain without alternation,[58] and keeps his explanation at the level of the eye as an organ. In this context a visual shape may be translated into terms of tensions of the eye[59] and various figures—circle, straight line, curved line—produce various movements of the optical muscles.[60] The perception of any space considered aesthetically awakens a tendency to move visual organs, and space may be defined as the possibility of such motion.

Continuing the identification of the physiological behavior of the optical organs with form, and going one stage beyond geometrical figures, Santayana considers the phenomenon of symmetry. The physiological basis of symmetry is the movement of the eye from side to side;[61] the formal basis of symmetry is a repetition of corresponding elements disposed in a unity wherein they are recognized and their repetition is expected.[62] The case of symmetry provides the evidence Santayana needs to continue the correlation of form with physiology. Symmetry implies that regularly repeated shapes confront the subject and perception of these shapes implies a predictable eye movement. Also there is something to be learned from the circumstance that the repeated shape taken in isolation is perceived differently from what it is in the combination made by its repetition.[63] Form is perception of a synthesis and the *raison d'être* of the synthesis is the relation of the sensible elements composing it.[64]

A crucial test for the presence of beauty from form is whether or not the valuing organism is aware of elements in the totality it is perceiving. If not, it is experiencing a sensation, not a perception of form.[65] Since perception of form occurs through awareness of elements, the same geometrical figure or the same example of symmetry conceivably could be an instance of beauty from form for one organism but not for another. For the organism which would perceive the figure or the symmetry while distinguishing the elements combined to produce it there would be value from form; for the organism which did not perceive combined elements there would be no value from form.[66]

The condition that combination of elements be recognized in value from form will require as great a variety of forms as there are kinds of variety in combining the elements constituting the completed form. Of these varieties Santayana enumerates three:[67] first, wherein the elements are all alike and the only diversity is numerical; second, wherein the elements differ and freely may be perceived in more than one order; and third, wherein the elements imply a predetermined organization.[68]

The first variety, that of combining elements which are all alike and whose only diversity is numerical, is radical and rudimentary. Its occurrence is identical with the perception of extension itself. To maintain that there is a perception of extension Santayana must presuppose that there is a sense and feeling of space, and further that the asserted feeling of space is a feeling of relation.[69] After he has instituted his feeling of relation in space or in extension, he is in a position to say that "the perception of extension is therefore a perception of form."[70] He admits perception of extension is a primitive sort of process but claims nevertheless that it may exist independently of other determination.[71] He states that the feeling derived from extension originates within the movements of the eye over an infinity of non-cognized positions or points. Such movement and exposure constitute a kind of raw sensing of multiplicity and continuity, leading to an emotion.[72] By reason of the presented points being considered as sensible elements synthesized into a quasi-totality with an accompanying emotion, Santayana obtains the conditions he requires for form and for aesthetic value as occurring under the aspect of bald extension.

Form as extension is quite distinct from form as contour,[73] and also from the material qualities objectified within extension.[74] But although distinct from material qualities, the formal effect of extension is specially adapted to alliance with them.[75]

A useful example of form from multiplicity in uniformity is a starry heaven. Besides being an actual instance of multiplicity in uniformity it has an immensity that conveys the idea of infinity. By the image of the heavens, considered according to physiological consequences, "every point in the retina is evenly excited and the local signs of all are simultaneously felt."[76] Emotion also occurs.[77] Moreover, each factor in the achievement of beauty from multiplicity in uniformity is enriched by sensuous and affective concomitants. The emotion affiliated with extension is reenforced by the emotion aroused by the stars.[78] The excitement from multiplicity without a subsequently recognizable image is intensified by the sensation of the countless distinct starry points; while the contrast of black firmament and vibrant white flecks supercharges the total impression,[79] which nevertheless, in its foundation, is a value from form as multiplicity in uniformity. However, in any value from form solely of this kind Santayana sees two main defects: first, it is unable to afford sustained interest as it inherently leads to monotony; and second, its opportunities for association are sharply limited.

The second of the varieties of form is that of elements which differ within themselves, and when perceived, are amenable to combination in more than one order. A distinctive characteristic of this variety of form is that it is utterly dependent on the faculty of apperception, under which formal types, assisting in perception, have been embedded in our mind. Santayana is quite explicit about the role of perception in the occurrence of beauty from form. The organism receives sensations which it formally combines and interprets, while the object stimulating the sensations is indeterminate. The mind itself assigns unstable forms to the indeterminate object. Since the object is indeterminate, its elements can be apperceived as forming numerous kinds of unities. The object arousing the reaction of form is indeterminate in the sense that each specific perception will be referred to an apperceptive norm as an ideal of the species.[80] But the apperceptive norm will vary according to two contexts: within the same individual the same perception could be referred fortuitously to different types, for example, the same outline of the same cloud could be perceived as both a camel and a whale[81] by the same individual; also among different individuals the apperception of form will vary merely by the condition that individual inventories of apperceptive types vary.[82]

Apperception is a free activity and accordingly functions most aptly when correlated with indeterminate objects to which it lends a variety of interests. Whatever external object is ambiguous because of the mode in which its elements are combined is the kind of object well suited to be assigned aesthetic value with the assistance of apperception.[83] The best analogy of the way apperception acts is furnished by the situation wherein an organism views a natural landscape. The landscape is given as indeterminate, as in the changing atmosphere, or masses of mountains, and the formal composition of it that results will use apperception for selection, emphasis, and grouping of elements. The result also will vary with the capacity of the individual for apperception, that is, with how abundantly his mind is stored with apperceptive types and what skill he possesses in applying types to physical things.[84]

Apperception of the presented indeterminate object is a process quite distinct from description of the object. In apperception the interest is in the object as part of the self; there is no interest in a neutrally descriptive report. Apperception takes place in the terms of the apperceiver, not in terms of the phenomenon apperceived; it is not an itemized record of characteristics of the object, but instead is a free interpretation of the object.[85] Apperception is a romanticism of form; paradoxically, it is a formal mastery of the formless. It produces a specific form in a context where no specific form is given: in Santayana's words, "the observer's own mind is the storehouse from which the beautiful form has to be drawn."[86] The object comes to the organism as if fluid and takes the shapes of the matrices the organism provides.

In visual form from apperception the elements combined are lines and movements in a certain proportion. The contour that results is viewed intrinsically and as stimulating the revival of some individual set of images, which is to say as leading to an act of recognition. It is the pleasure released by the act of recognition that constitutes the beauty in this variety of form.[87] The faculty of apperception, then, receives the given single percept on the basis of such formal elements as line, movement, and proportion. In so receiving these elements there is called up from the mind's reservoir of images some set suggested by the given percept. Recognition occurs, with or without pleasure. In the cases where pleasure accompanies the recognition, beauty from form is achieved.

The aesthetic value following the stimulus to the apperceptive act depends on the character already acquired by the ideal type evoked.[88] Recognition alone is not sufficient to assure the required pleasure. Nor is the prime condition for pleasure found in what the type intrinsically may be; rather it is in the adaptability of the type to the given individual mind. The form itself does not give pleasure. It merely forecasts pleasure that will eventuate if there is preestablished affinity between the type and the individual percipient.[89] But a still more decisive factor in producing the aesthetic value is the relation of the particular impression to the type.[90] To the extent that the impression is a rich or sympathetic embodiment of the ideal contained within the experiencing organism the recognition is pleasurable and aesthetic value follows; to the extent that the given impression falls short of congruity with the ideal there is cerebral discord and failure to gain aesthetic value.

The formation of the type so crucial to aesthetic value from apperception is a consequence of repeated experiencing of an individual thing, without however being a calculated average of these experiences.[91] Not only perceptual, but also emotional and other irrational factors will influence deviation from the average.[92] This subjective distortion has the consequence of making degrees of beauty depend on each individual nature. Each organism makes its own scale of aesthetic values and beauty from this variety of form becomes entirely relative.[93] The given object which is indeterminate in form is also indeterminate in respect to value. Both the form and the value coincident with the indeterminate presentation reside in the mind of the observer.[94]

The third and last variety of form is that in which the elements are given as combined, so that a combination does not have to be made by universal retinal punctual sensation as in the first variety, nor from a stock of apperceptive types as in the second variety. In the third variety the combination is furnished in a completed state, as when the organism is confronted with a work of art or with something presented by physical nature: what is given is determinate as form and is located within a real or natural object. Literature is another example of determinate form. In literature significance is conveyed by the form and order of words,[95] not by words as sensuous material. Literature cannot be literature and still be formally indeterminate.[96]

In contrast with the case of the indeterminate presentation, which was not a new object and did not in-form the mind but instead aroused an apperceptive response, the case of presentation of a determined organization of data compels the eye and imagination to follow new paths and see new relations. The synthesis of elements is given rather than obtained subjectively from an apperceptive type called up at random. This third variety of form is form already brought to its final status. As in nature and art there has been discrimination and precision operating beforehand and no endowment of the sensed real object with previously unspecified forms is required; also reverie is superfluous and the emotional content of the experience has a different density and color. Most physical objects represent a system of atoms already formally arranged and not depending on a selection of a type by the percipient as specifying its organization.[97] The determinate organization of the real object itself is also the first step toward the production of the mind's apperceptive forms.[98] To a large extent nature is the mediator or supplier of all apperceptive forms to the experiencing organism, and artists, as fabricators of determined form in their works, have to return to nature for fresh forms when existing ones, after a period of inspired interpretation by a master, degenerate into academic, conventional, or unimaginative productions.[99]

The fact that nature furnishes a determined form raises the question as to whether nature follows a principle in combining the elements in the given unity or form. The answer is yes and the principle involved is one of utility.[100] The shape of the pyramid is an example: this shape proves its stability by withstanding disrupting forces and because of that kind of utility becomes a type in nature that may be imitated by builders.[101] Art forms follow natural forms and the principle of utility is active in both. Yet although utility may determine in a large measure nature's formal organizations, it does not determine to the same extent the value of beauty from the completed forms.[102] Retinal and muscular tensions influence the pleasure of the response to form. Also a gradation of abstract forms is possible, with rank according to aesthetic value and independent utility.[103]

But beauty from a determined abstract spatial and linear organization is an advanced stage in aesthetic valuation. As art evolves it is beautiful by the sensuousness of its material and ornamentation before it pleases by its formal organization; and before either it was simply a useful form. The point of maximum satisfaction is attained when the interest in form is emphasized by an interest in the accompanying ornament.[104]

Santayana views form as a synthesis of sensible elements or qualities. This synthesis has three modes: it may be entirely determined, indeterminate, or partially determined. In multiplicity in uniformity the synthesis is determined, but only partially, since it does not include more than optical physiology. In a panorama of nature, for example, of clouds, haze, or water, the synthesis is indeterminate; in most objects of nature and art the synthesis is entirely determined. The pleasure arising from each kind of synthesis and simultaneously objectified is Santayana's value from form.

4. *Value from Expression*

In Santayana's account of the occurrence of the value, beauty, he presupposes a sense of beauty as given within the organism. Although he mentions different aspects of this sense, he considers it as empirically indivisible and as always acting as a single simple thing.[105] Altogether he distinguishes three aspects of its behavior. The first was its response to sensible material and the second its response to abstract form. Both of these excitements had as a referend something intrinsic to the presentation. In the third aspect, the response of the sense of beauty, with its corresponding value, is stimulated by something extrinsic to the presentation, by some other experience which the presentation suggests. The value takes place with respect to an expression of the presentation, not with respect to the presentation itself; and the basis for the expression is the mental process of association.

When value from sensible material was distinguished, the impulse toward pleasure acted immediately, quite apart from other psychological connections; when value from form was distinguished the impulse to pleasure was still active, but had to be cleared through a synthesis of sensational elements. In distinguishing value through expression the impulse to pleasure is again basic but directs itself to something outside of the object's material and formal properties, and the value forthcoming requires the extra step of association: expression is a quality acquired by objects through association, a meaning and tone characteristic of other objects, but merged in a given object which is otherwise independent.[106] However, the pleasure objectified by association remains an immediate feeling.[107]

Presupposed in expression, then, are two objects: the given and the associated, plus an emotional effect originating in the associated object. Further, expression has the capacity of acting in two ways: it "may make beautiful by suggestion things in themselves indifferent, or it may come to heighten the beauty which they already possess."[108]

Expression resembles material and formal value in being a pleasurable physiological radiation of a given stimulus and in going through the assumed process of objectification,[109] but expression differs from material and formal value in being the survival of an innate experience in the manner of a habit, rather than the reaction of an innate disposition in the manner of an instinct. A more conspicuous difference is that material and formal value occur with reference to only one term or object whereas expression implies two: "the first is the object actually presented—the word, the image, the expressive thing; the second is the object suggested—the further thought, emotion, or image evoked, the thing expressed."[110]

However, for Santayana, expression is definitely not a theory of association by external relation.[111] Like his general theory of beauty, his theory of expression is distinguished by being restricted to the operation within an individual mind.[112] This relativism in expression is unavoidable for it is the individual mind that must supply one of the terms used in the association; there is no public presentation of the associated object. The value from expression will arise when an emotion of pleasure surrounds the thing expressed, yet the beauty of expression is not in the least separate from the expressive thing.[113] Aesthetic value accrues to the given object, but it does so not on the basis of perceived qualities of the given object but instead on the basis of experiences associated with it.

Santayana's doctrine of association as the foundation of aesthetic expression permits something non-aesthetic to contribute to something aesthetic. In his distinction of a first and second term, the first term, or presented object, is invariably aesthetic, but the second term, or associated object, is free to stand for other kinds of experience: for utility, for cost, for economy and fitness, or for evil and pain. Utility that will heighten the pleasure in the presented object[114] may appear as a piece of interesting information, a theory, a satisfaction of a curiosity, or otherwise. Cost is effective[115] when interpreted as rarity, as distinction, or as exceptional craft. Economy of arrangement and fitness of form, especially as found in architecture, are expressions that enhance the presented object. Utility, cost, economy, and fitness as attributes of the second term may react on the first term to reinforce it aesthetically, while the negative values such as evil, pain, and pathos may be diminished by being contemplated with the assistance of art.[116]

The relief of pain and tolerance of evil by transmission through an aesthetic medium may serve as a basis for a theory of tragedy. According to this theory, situations, the components of which are terrifying and painful if beheld as literal, discrete events, are softened and beautified by the artist's hand. The artist creates within a form which inspires a beauty that encompasses the literally tragic situation. The resulting value of beauty conquers evil by making it become a pleasing experience beyond its literal status as a painful experience.[117] Santayana opens a vista wherein tragedy may be seen as implying two layers: the first being the literal situation, bare and untouched by the art of the drama; the second being the portrayal of the same situation, with the artist's imagination and the instrumentality of dramatic form combating the given evil impressions. There then arises a sort of conflict between the pain occasioned by the raw event and the pleasure afforded by the artist's vision. If the situation had been left on the unimaginative level the unaesthetic forces would conquer; by the entrance of the power of the poet's imagination, his skill in formal construction, and the expression of truth that is mixed with both, the aesthetic side is the victor. Such a theory of tragedy is one aspect of Santayana's theory of expression, the aspect wherein a negative value in the second term is transformed into a positively agreeable association by the expressiveness of the first term.

In the production of the aesthetic effect of objects the principal influence is the total emotional value of the given individual consciousness. The value is attributed to the object by a projection which provides the illusion of objectivity of beauty. This value is not exclusively inherent in the perception of the object; it may be the result of the formation of other ideas, evoked by the perception. It is then beauty of expression and its range is broad. It may be implicated in the idea of utility, of cost, of economy and fitness, also in tragedy and comedy, in wit and humor, in the good and the true, and in the comprehensive and sublime.

In summary, Santayan's doctrines of aesthetic experience emerge from an associationist, functional psychology, conjoined with a hedonistic value theory, in the setting of a mechanistic universe. Beauty is a value experience, non-cognitive and constituted by an objectification of pleasure. The experience presupposes a sense of beauty within the percipient. Beauty occurs in the presence of elements of phenomenal objects distinguishable as sensible material, abstract form, and associated qualites, although beauty itself has no elements. The factor of sensible material involves the perceptual processes of sight and hearing together with the organism's vital impulses; the factor of form involves a perception of a synthesis of sensible elements separately apprehended; the factor of expression involves the association of an absent object with the experience of the presented object. Under all three conditions, considered both individually and in aggregate, a process originating in desire becomes pleasure; the act of objectification follows and the pleasure becomes an illusion of a quality of a thing. Thereby pleasure becomes beauty.

CHAPTER III

Poetry and Criticism

■

1. *Preliminary Considerations*

Santayana's thought in the field of art and aesthetics, as elsewhere, is characterized by a fairly distinctive pattern of development. Within his writings the growth and elaboration of any given topic takes place between two points, one an initial embryonic structure of subjective conviction and the other a well-wrought, theoretically defensible exposition. The temporal interval between these two points varies with the topic; neither this interval nor the sequence of topics conform to any kind of predetermined regulation. The unfolding of initial insights is not a conscious operation in accordance with some rational ordering or other logic. The situation appears to be rather that the earliest stages of Santayana's thinking simultaneously embraced a variety of *aperçus* and that these were given explicit statement in some larger form after a seemingly fortuitous span of time. One mark which distinguishes Santayana from many other philosophers is that almost the entire subject matter of his lifetime of writing was adumbrated, at least thematically, before the more elaborate public record of it was made. In at least two other respects he is distinctive in handling theoretical material: first, he does not generate new convictions nor discover new paths of investigation as he goes along; and, second, even though there are instances where he has modified some of his theories, he does not advance his thought by persistent alteration of something he already has written, nor by piecemeal addition of a superstructure to foundations already formulated. At its source each of Santayana's works is on a par with the others. From a common starting point, members of an original nucleus of diverse convictions are given full statement at some unpredictable later date. It is to this kind of pattern Santayana refers when he says there is nothing in all of his philosophy that was not implicit in his early poems.[1]

In the embryonic domain shared by all of Santayana's subsequently explicit viewpoints were glimmerings of the insights that later came to light in his writings on aspects of art and aesthetics. The beliefs concerning aesthetic experience were the first to emerge to full growth, but constantly stirring beside them were the theories of criticism and of the active part taken by the aesthetic contribution to the moral life. Almost all of Santayana's theory of aesthetic experience was set forth in one work, *The Sense of Beauty*. His theory of rational art was concentrated in *Reason in Art* with supplementary treatment in other volumes of *The Life of Reason*. His expression relating to poetry and criticism was the most diffuse, spreading over four works, published between 1890 and 1910: "Walt Whitman: a Dialogue," 1890; *Interpretations of Poetry and Religion*, 1900; "What Is Aesthetics?", 1904; *Three Philosophical Poets*, 1910.[2] The central and most comprehensive treatment of Santayana's theory of criticism is the collection of essays published under the title *Interpretations of Poetry and Religion*. Arbitrarily considered, with the objective of extracting the theory of criticism contained in this volume, the subject matter of the essays roughly falls into three divisions: the first concerns the establishment of the interrelation of poetry and religion; the second outlines the psychological functions pertinent to poetry and religion; and the third exhibits the components and the scope of poetry together with a normative hierarchy for critical judgments. The first of these divisions is influenced by certain nineteenth-century opinion that asserted the similarity between secular literature and the sacred doctrinal writing, in particular by Matthew Arnold's stand on this question.[3] As Santayana in *The Sense of Beauty* had produced his own version of James's, Ebbinghaus', Fechner's, and Lipps's psychology, Lotze's ethics, and other nineteenth-century scientific views, so in *Interpretations of Poetry and Religion* he produces his own version of Arnold's criticism.[4] The second division deals with the individual's psychological faculties in a way that is equivalent to an extension of the psychological basis of aesthetic experience in *The Sense of Beauty*. In this earlier work the focus of attention was the mechanism by which pleasure was generated to become a value; in *Interpretations of Poetry and Religion* there is an account of the psychological factors affecting aesthetic criticism and creation. The third division is the most pivotal to the critical side of Santayana's aesthetics: it is a statement of the scale by which relative rank may be assigned to different examples of poetry. This scale is a consequence of the belief that poetry and religion are interrelated. Such a belief lends support to the claim that as an imaginative projection poetry is coextensive with religion and also that poetry with a moral function takes precedence over poetry without one. The structure, then, of Santayana's theory of poetry and its criticism is composed of three interlocking elements: a specified psychology of understanding and imagination, a doctrine of kinship of poetry and religion, and a schema for measuring poetic accomplishment.

2. *Stages of Imagination*

The virtual identification of poetry and religion by Santayana is dependent on his account of the understanding and imagination. Under the kind of psychological terms he proposes poetry and religion may be identified and their mutual character used for the ends of literary criticism; with another kind of psychology this overlapping of poetry and religion might not ensue.

In the psychology endorsed by Santayana there are two kinds of imagination, one denoted by the imagination itself and the other by the understanding.[5] He denies any exclusive disjunction between these two psychic functions. They are continuous and any differentiation of them is nominal. These conclusions about imagination and understanding are drawn from a carefully wrought theory of mental organization. In Santayana's view only two of the five senses produce understanding.[6] These are hearing and sight. Of the two, sight has the dominant role. It is visual apprehension that activates the mind's powers of "synthesis, abstraction, reproduction, invention,"[7] and these powers Santayana takes to be equivalent to understanding. However, understanding has a companion faculty in the form of the imagination, which asserts itself almost as soon as the understanding begins to function. At this point, says Santayana, "the mind . . . turns from the frigid problems of observation to its own visions."[8] The understanding interprets the senses but the imagination always "overlays that interpretation."

The assumption whereby in mental processes the imagination inevitably joins forces with the understanding serves Santayana as a valuable premise. From it he may conclude that the imagination does the work of the intelligence and assert that "imagination and intelligence do not differ in their origin but only in their validity."[9] There is, then, a relationship among common sense, science, and imagination. They are alike in source, in character, and in motivation.[10] They differ only in respect to validity. On the basis of their similarity Santayana can maintain that there is no material or efficient distinction among them but only an ideal one; common sense, science, and imagination, though they may be shown to have independent functions under logical discrimination, are inseparable as to function in their dynamic state.[11] Santayana now may proclaim a distinction most useful to his doctrine of poetry and religion and to other of his literary and philosophical views: "Those conceptions which, after they have spontaneously arisen, prove serviceable in practice, and capable of verification in sense, we call ideas of the understanding. The others remain ideas of the imagination."[12]

Having assured himself of the kinship of understanding and imagination and accomplished differentiation of the two by means of the criterion of utility and verification by sense, Santayana has reached the point where he may impose a ranking on various individual minds. The norm for this ranking is susceptibility to imagination as it relates to the large questions of life and the universe. Santayana regards the highest order of mind as that wherein imagination envisions states of affairs that are beyond the scope of the understanding.[13] In this kind of metavista there is also present feeling and passion that provide further distinction from the process of ordinary understanding.[14] Santayana now has demarcated a sphere of imagination not available to understanding, a sort of elite territory that imagination alone may enter. It is in this sphere that religion and metaphysics arise. Both of these disciplines, as well as poetry, require apprehension of supersensible forms.[15] Paradoxically it is "the intuitions which science could not use"[16] that remain to be the inspiration of poetry and religion.

Prophecy or revelation become synonyms for imagination and signify that somehow creations of the imagination have correlation

with an ultimate truth.[17] There is here a slight implication that
other kinds of imaginative reports do not achieve the same status
with respect to truth as found in prophecy or revelation. There is
however no development of this implied dichotomy among imaginative acts.

The property of being prophecy is made the means of strength-
ening the mutual interpenetration of the understanding and the
imagination. In function both are primarily prophetic;[18] nevethe-
less they exhibit secondary differences in the matters of verification
and of use. Prophecies of the understanding are verifiable within the
operation of ordinary sense perception; prophecies of the higher
imagination may not be. Also prophecies of the understanding may
serve to warrant success in practical action, whereas prophecies of
the higher imagination carry no such warrant.[19] The prophecies of
the understanding relate to established kinds of experience shared
within most human communities and verifiable within the sense
experience of the given community. Accordingly prophecies of the
understanding frequently are put to use in the advancement of
general welfare.[20] The prophecies of higher imagination overreach
the level of common experience to the extent that they are not easily
and quickly verified, and hence are not easily and quickly shared.
However, indirectly, and after allowance for a period of infiltration
and contemplation, the conceptions of the free imagination may be
of more use than those of the kind of imagination which is restricted
to the understanding.[21] Throughout his presentation Santayana
assumes that the bare property of being visionary is possessed to an
equal degree by imagination limited to the exercise of understanding and imagination not thus delimited. Both segments of the range
of imagination are alike in their function of envisioning; they differ
in respect to consequences from the phenomenal objects produced.

Santayana is emphatic about the point that, in spite of the lack
of immediate utilitarian results, the free imagination is, in the long
view, a source of huge benefit. He extols free imagination as "the
great unifier of humanity" and urges its exercise as a personally
salutary measure.[22] Yet as a reservation to his glowing eulogy he
mentions the hazard of irresponsibility and treachery that acts of
imagination may conceal.[23] At whatever level it operates, free in
itself or restricted by understanding, it is a function of imagination
to transform what is unknowable into a symbol. In this function the
understanding, as a representative of imagination, is no better than

a dream. Santayana wants to be clear that our senses, the instruments of our understanding, are as "human, as 'subjective' as our wills."[24] Nevertheless the utilitarian value of all these products of human ideation, whatever their species in imagination, exhibits great disparity. With respect to human purposes and demands all symbols produced by imagination are not on a par.[25] But with the differences due to utilitarian valuation excluded, ideas of restricted imagination, which is to say ideas of understanding, and ideas of free imagination are of one piece.

3. *Poetry, Religion, and Standards of Criticism*

Santayana now has the psychological foundation and the discrimination within the sphere of imagination to enable him to defend a belief in the essential identity of poetry and religion, which is the uppermost single idea in all of his literary philosophy and criticism. Poetry and religion are ideal constructions that make the facts of nature and history morally intelligible and practically important.[26] The supreme function of the imagination is moral and expresses itself in poetry and religion.

In basic texture poetry and religion are the same. They are substantially one and acquire different names according to whether either is embodied in life or kept merely superposed upon it.[27] "Religion" is preferred when the reference is to a principle used in the conduct of life; when there is no such pragmatic association "poetry" is chosen.[28] But in neither case is a change in the imaginative content denoted. It is understood that all manifestations of religion are not of equal moral significance and the same is so with respect to all manifestations of poetry. It is when the intuition of each attains its maximum comprehension of reality that their identification with each other is most complete.[29]

With poetry and religion conceived as perfect counterparts of each other, Santayana has a ready-made standard for literary criticism. The highest ranking poetry will be that which achieves the religious mode in scope, refinement, and profundity. Other poetry, perforce, must accept a lower rank.

In formulating his scale for judging poetry, Santayana designates three levels of analysis. The three levels contain four stages of ascending rank, the lower level having two of these, the intermediate and upper level having one each.

The two stages found on the lower level are those of euphony and euphuism. Euphony is the lower of the two and as a criterion asks only that the sound of poetry be pure, pleasing, and fluid. At the next higher stage, euphuism, there is a demand for coherence in imagery together with associations in memory and suggestions for imaginative constructions from elliptical phrasing, with all these elements forming a harmonious unity.[30] The third stage occupies the intermediate level, and to qualify for this rank the poet must inject himself into his poetry. In so doing he will be classed as romantic and be free to disregard categories that maintain purely rational order.[31] At the fourth stage, or highest level, reason must be reintroduced and the scope of the imaginative outlook extended so that the subject matter selected may be treated on a cosmic scale.[32] The poetry of the lowest level is a kind dominated by sensuous surface and purveying pleasantness merely by response to demands of the ear. The poetry of the intermediate level has the additional feature of romantic deflections of the self or idealizations of episodes in human existence. The poetry of the highest level is rational over a background of universal proportions and has its beauty from its religious response to demands from the soul.

4. Psychological Features of Poetic Creation

Besides the bare structure of levels which Santayana designs for grading poetry, he specifies some characteristics that will be found in all poetry regardless of the rank it might earn. These characteristics are what might be called poetic content, and this distinctive kind of content may be viewed in terms of its origins, its substantial nature, and its function. Poetic content, or stuff, has its source in emotional experience. As an emotional expression it may be seen most clearly by contrasting it with an intellectual expression. Viewed in the light of the self's experience, the real world is only an outline, superimposed on the dreamlike state of the soul which perpetually is one of chaos and unrest.[33] There are, then, two sides to the contact between the soul and the outer world, and these sides are different in kind. One resembles a top surface character- ized by having a logical and intellectual order; the other is an under surface of dreaming, generating, amorphous becoming that makes no use of logical methods in its thought products yet always has discursive reason imminent above it.[34] This subrational layer of experience is the soil of the emotional expression required in poetry.[35] In the case of the ordinary man this obscure region may be the antecedent of merely insignificant utterance; but in the case of the poet it is the source and efficient cause of his art.

The substance of poetry, however, is gleaned out of an interaction between the mind's emotional and intellectual divisions. Left to itself the nature of the intellect is to cast out any emotion that tinges a perception. The intellect strives to arrogate control and to impose its own conditions on perceptual material. In many cases it succeeds. But the poet will not tolerate this kind of usurpation. He retains the emotion that the intellect would have banished[36] and allows it to permeate his ideas while he gives them imaginative interpretation, under the stimulation of his sense of beauty and his impulse to harmony.[37] Within this poetic act the substance and chief ingredient is emotion. Whatever the imagination projects, wherever the poet's dream is directed, it is emotion that is the common binder of all his creation and it is emotion that takes him out of the province of discursive reason.[38] For the poet those things hold together that have among them the property of having adherence to the same emotions. This principle which enlists emotion for coloring the constituents of poetry with the same tone distinguishes poetic thought from the practical kind which holds together on account of some given interest and from the scientific kind which holds together on account of spatio-temporal relations or identity of theoretical formulation.[39]

Besides indicating the source and substance of poetry, Santayana mentions its function. The poet's creations are not merely diversion or whimsy; they have an established function. As might be expected this function is moral in character. To grasp its import one must imagine a bidirectional movement on the part of the poet's creative faculty. In one phase the movement penetrates beneath common perceptual experience and embraces the raw stuff of sensation with unfettered imagination. In the other phase the movement transcends these depths of indefiniteness and forms novel compositions that lift it above the dead level of plain, uninspired experience.[40] Here Santayana distinguishes two essential steps[41] traversed by the poet: the going downward into a state of unintellectualized sensation where the poet has for companions what literally might be called madmen and the going upward into a state of reason and the company of enlightened prophets. The first step is for the objective of obtaining materials to be converted to higher ends; the second is to form those ends in a structure of symbols representing the truest aims and finest achievements of the soul.[42] The two steps are immediately preceded by a sort of intuitive decision that customary perceptual behavior will be superseded and the poetic plunge to immersion in the bare roots of sensation and imagination will be made. Santayana aptly calls this antecedent awareness the "plastic moment."

In Santayana's view all operations of the mind are unified in a standard way, and accordingly there will be a close correspondence of the mechanics of mental functioning in all individuals. It follows that the mental products denoted as science and those denoted as common sense go through the same process as those known as poetry. On Santayana's premises the diverse results of these three categories have the same mental acts preceding them. They analyze, they find their material in experience, and they use the material found to fabricate a moral ideal.[43] Each is continuous with the other in the sense of using the same process, the same order of procedure, and the same goal;[44] the single point at which they differ is in the material selected for processing.[45]

Common sense implies a prosaic outlook and experience limited to its terms acquires a prosaic character. One of the higher tasks of poetry is to alter the drab character of non-poetic experience by infusing it with "a rhythm more congenial and intelligible to the mind."[46] Another unique aspect of poetry is its preference for images and emotions disregarded by practical thinking in both its common sense and scientific versions. These rejected images and emotions are embraced by the poetic enterprise which ironically produces a result that is more faithful to the original experience than is provided by either common sense or practical science. That is, given any experience, science and common sense select the phenomenal ingredients they will process to their kind of conclusions. They delete associations of emotion and also various images discriminated as being superfluous to cognition or other formulation. However, the very emotions and images unfit for science or common sense are seized upon by the poetic operation and the poetic outcome corresponds to the given experience more truly than any report offered by science or common sense.[47]

Although Santayana is willing to construct levels for gradation of the poetic product that serve as standards for its criticism and as categories determining its type, he never confuses this normative attitude towards poetry with the factual data of the human poetic matrix. Regardless of whether poetry after the fact is separable into graded compartments, in principle all poetry is alike.[48] All poetry evolves out of the same substance, which is emotion, and from the same center, which is the passions.[49] On the respective questions, then, of inclusion under a principle, of the context of origin, and of the nature of fundamental substance, all poetry is one. It is on questions of critical judgment of the finished poetic product of individual artists that poetry appears diverse.

It remains to be noted that it is impossible to produce poetry through the agency of either the imagination or the passions acting alone.[50] Nor can there be any such state of affairs as might be called artistic voluntarism, for the will has no part in the creation of ideas.[51] It is the senses and experience of the outer world that are crucial to the poetic art simply because they are the sole providers of the ideas needed to keep the soul from being empty.[52] In spite of its emotional substance and irrational origin, poetry fits the world and practical living. For poetry, in its ideal aspects, cannot survive unless it is supported by sensation and cognition of the outer world.[53] Furthermore, if visionary comprehension of the real be considered as the summit of an individual's development, then one may infer that poetry is an educating force. It is possible that Santayana here thought of it as the greatest educating force.

5. Early Critical Tendencies

While *Interpretations of Poetry and Religion* is the major statement of Santayana's conclusions concerning criticism, two articles published separately, one preceding and the other following it, disclose the considerable reflection that he had given to broad issues confronting the critic seeking principles to support his opinions. The earlier article is titled, "Walt Whitman: a Dialogue"[54] and the later one "What Is Aesthetics?"[55]

"Walt Whitman: a Dialogue" is excellent evidence of the extent to which criticism occupied Santayana's mind at an early point in his career. While this work is brief, it is profuse in exhibition of questions, the answers to which would be pivotal in establishing a trend of critical effort. Sagely, Santayana does not provide the answers. He apparently is struggling to clarify a position for himself without becoming conclusive about it. The dialogue contains two fictional participants, Van Tender and McStout. Van Tender roughly corresponds to a protagonist and McStout to his antagonist.

Van Tender is liberal and romantic. He proposes a theory wherein individual interpretation is a prime factor in poetry. The poet's own feeling-tones and purely sensuous expression are sufficient sanction for poetic merit, and freely imaginative expression of the unique and the momentary without reference to any accepted external standard is entirely proper.

McStout is fashionably conservative. He opposes his friend with an academic and even puritanical version of the classic imitation theory, according to which the poet will represent or reproduce some generally accepted truth. However, in McStout's conception, the truth does not happen to be an *arche* but is merely what is believed to be best according to the prescriptions of convention.

The two men are immersed in a large issue that frequently has arisen in the history of criticism. In a way they are reviving the old conflict over art according to nature or art according to rules, another statement of which may be the question: is art an imitation or an interpretation of life; is it fundamental to art to depict the instinctive, immediate flux, or to be guided by the integrating force of rational discipline? Throughout the discussion, the poetry of Walt Whitman is merely a convenient illustration of the principles in dispute. There are much larger points at stake than whether or not Whitman is adequate as a poet.

Actually the main issue of imitation *vs.* interpretation is not explicitly pressed during the dialogue but rather is superordinate to the examination of a number of sub-issues. These, if resolved, would assist in partially clearing the more comprehensive issue in which they are contained. These smaller explicit issues, all germane to poetry, include questions regarding linguistics, conformity to convention, necessity of illusion, communication of feeling, communication of an outer beauty, variation in the intrinsic beauty of objects, standards of valuing, and moral consequences. No settlement is reached on any of these questions.

Van Tender begins by suggesting that the objective of poetry is the production of a feeling of pleasure as a response of the reader. He believes this objective is consistent with the evidence that men innately are equipped to experience this feeling of pleasure and that the poet is able to transfer this feeling by reason of his unique capacity for absorbing and reinterpreting the transient processes of physical nature.[56] The poetry of Whitman will confirm this view.

McStout does not deny Van Tender's point but relegates it to secondary significance and classification as an amusing variation from authentic poetic production. McStout's criterion for slighting Van Tender is propriety in the use of words, and Whitman provides the example of a failure to satisfy this criterion.

Van Tender will not yield to the criterion of propriety in language for he believes it conceals an ambiguity. For him there are two kinds of propriety: one academic and artificial; the other natural and popular.[57]

McStout admits there are both kinds of linguistic propriety but says that fact in no way upsets his criterion since the kind of language he is rejecting is one arbitrarily invented, having neither vernacular nor philological propriety.[58]

Van Tender refuses to make any form of linguistic convention a fixed requirement for poetry on the ground that the achievement of emotional effects from the poet's distinctive language justifies its use and supersedes conformity to any public or scholarly mode of utterance.[59]

McStout now shifts his position. He will disregard the linguistic issue but substitute for it what he considers a larger one: the question of the indispensability of standards and the absurdity of mere originality.[60] In other words, McStout will uphold orthodoxy of all kinds.

Van Tender admits that if one is chronically committed to academic models a barbarism is annoying. But he contends this objection is outweighed by the interest competent barbaric writing stimulates. The stylistic barbarian is able to satisfy desires and inspire his readers to a degree beyond what is found in the work of the purist. McStout disagrees. He believes that inspiration is contingent on a certain amount of understanding and that the best poetry contains a thought sequence affording a comprehension not found in barbarians like Whitman.[61]

Van Tender replies that poetry is not expected to supply a theory or description of things, but that Whitman's ability to arouse an attitude of appreciation for the objects he enumerates is something well suited to verse.[62] McStout's answer is subtle but illuminating. It is one of the most incisive bits of thought in the dialogue and rests on the distinction between poetry and science.[63] Whitman is deficient because he refers to an external object in the literal manner of science, whereas the true poet presents objects not literally but in a state of illusion covered by an imaginative glamour.[64] Here Mc-Stout seems to abandon his character as a champion of academic regulation and to veer toward Van Tender's convictions about poetic license and originality.

Van Tender then makes wholesale charges that all of McStout's views are false because he persists in approaching poetry through the medium of definition. For Van Tender this kind of approach must fail, because the truth of poetry is never in any theory but lies solely in the concrete perception and emotion that poetry stimulates.[65] As for McStout's thought that the poet furnishes a glamorous garment of illusion for the objects included in his discourse, Van Tender argues that it is not poetic artistry that purveys illusion. Rather, illusion is something already fixed in objects by habit and custom. He believes that the criterion for beauty is a perception of a feeling of fitness and necessity but that beauty is everywhere and requires only the genius of the poet to give it manifestation.[66]

McStout's reaction is ingenious. He asserts that if beauty is everywhere, then literary tradition is arbitrary and could originate by blind chance. He does not believe beauty is ubiquitous and claims the poet must discover something in itself beautiful. A condition of this discovery is that it will take place in one setting rather than another and will involve a selection of the beautiful from among many things that are not.

Van Tender is hard put to retort to McStout's statement. He admits that intrinsic worth is present in the object the poet selects as material of beauty but adds that from the act of selection of certain material it does not follow that beauty is not everywhere. It merely indicates that what the poet selects happens to suit his momentary needs better than what he abjures. Intrinsic worth is in all of nature, if one looks about with complete exclusion of selfish motives. A sort of aesthetic justice prevails in our environment. When individual psychology is suppressed, intrinsic worth is discernible everywhere.[67]

McStout's reply is unique. To hold his position he invokes the ancient epistemological doctrine of Empedocles that "like knows like" and uses it as a threat to admiration without discrimination. If we admire every object, as Whitman is willing to do, and beasts happen to be among the objects frequently admired, then we may come to resemble these beasts. To avoid this consequence McStout recommends the adoption of standards that will make poetry represent "the better instincts of man."

Van Tender quickly charges that McStout is now taking the discussion out of the field of poetry and placing it in that of morality. His opponent agrees that there is a moral aspect to what he says but believes that it is warranted, because all acts, including that of writing poetry, have consequences, and as soon as consequences are discussed the field of morals is entered.[68]

Van Tender then maintains that the poet is an observer and not a performer. Accordingly he does not belong under a moral category. The observer of an act does not participate in the act, and the only moral consequences that concern the poet come about indirectly. The poet, like the gods, continually observes both good and evil and thereby acquires a knowledge of life that gives him an advantage in the conduct of it.[69]

McStout's defense grows weaker, but he does not yield completely. He notes that observation never can be a substitute for action and that if the poet's nature be restricted to that of the rapturous observer, then the poet as a poet is unable to engage in morally worthy deeds.[70]

Van Tender completes Santayana's early venture in aesthetic criticism by observing that when the poet perceives the beauty of the world he helps other men perceive the same phenomenon. Here the poet performs an act of widening human sympathies, reconciling men with nature and other human beings, and promoting understanding and tolerance.[71] It is an example of a moral act through the agency of the poet's contemplation and seems not only to nullify McStout's contrary view but also to be divergent from how Van Tender himself had previously viewed the moral consequences of poetry.

This dialogue, by an examination of contrary viewpoints, seeks to discover the scope and nature of poetry. Santayana, with thorough deliberation, wavers between issues. He prefers to question rather than to solve: Shall he award the classicist or the romanticist the laurels? Is poetic art an imitation or interpretation of the universe and its constitution? Is the best poetry instinctive, passionate, and representative of the flux of existence or must poetry bring itself under some ideal discipline? Is fact or value to be the prior consideration? Is emotion to supersede thought? In one kind of criticism poetry may be seen as something that is liberal, passive, tolerant, and contemplative; in another kind it may be seen as orthodox, selective, and judicial. The treatment of all these questions is, by Santayana's choice, suggestive, not conclusive.

6. *The Anomaly of Aesthetics*

Consistent with his native ability and extensive practice in the field of aesthetics Santayana was well aware of the obstacles to any adequate definition of this discipline. In "What Is Aesthetics?" he skillfully probes the elements comprising these obstacles. This article has a twofold merit: first, it brings forward many of the conceptual conflicts that the label, aesthetics, chronically conceals; and, second, it outlines some principles fundamental to aesthetic criticism. Santayana seeks to either circumscribe or define aesthetics and finds the enterprise fraught with difficulties. On the basis of the unresolved issues he encounters, he concludes that the question he faces is without an answer. But before arriving at this opinion he contributes several penetrating and enlightening observations.

To some extent Santayana indicates a predisposition to be negative toward his topic for he begins by remarking that some questions "are insoluble and merely vexatious, because the terms they are stated in already traduce and dislocate the constitution of things."[72] The implication is that purely aesthetic questions belong in this category, and the word "aesthetics" is almost belittled as "a loose term lately applied in academic circles to everything that has to do with works of art or with the sense of beauty."[73]

In his search for a unique and authentic domain of aesthetics, Santayana begins with a consideration of whether or not aesthetics may be identified with some distinct activity. But this avenue quickly closes by leading to heterogeneity: an art student carries on aesthetic activity, so does a psychologist in a laboratory. A restriction to the category of aesthetic activity as thinking brings no better result: a dialectician concerned with the relation of the beautiful to the rational or to the absolutely good is speculating aesthetically; so is a theologian concerned with the emanation of the Holy Ghost from the Son and from the Father, when the Holy Ghost signifies a fulness of life realized in beauty.

Historical and literary accidents, it seems, have been responsible for the association of the word aesthetics with a group of disparate activities, including any flattering of an individual consciousness by its phantasmagoria or any detection of some intrinsic value for perception.[74] As a consequence there is an aggregate of miscellaneous aesthetic occasions but within them no specific aesthetic quality is discoverable, whether it be sought in nature, in an organ of sense, or in the sphere of spirit. Moreover, aesthetic experience has two inherent characteristics that are bound to lead to variegated manifestations: it is broad and it is incidental. Accordingly it invites and admits widely divergent interpretations.[75]

Santayana next turns his attention to the relation of reasoned knowledge and aesthetics. Reasoned knowledge may proceed along two lines, either in conjunction with observation or with dialectic. Reason and observation produce natural science; reason and dialectic produce ideal science. The question is: how does aesthetics fit into these operations of reasoned knowledge? The answer seems to be that aesthetics straddles the dichotomy and is partially in both natural science and ideal science. Aesthetic subject matter like the phenomena of art and taste is factual and an object for natural history, natural science, and empirical philosophy; subject matter like creative effort and intent in poetic composition or in critical interpretation is ideal and belongs in a realm of value.[76] So again aesthetics is ambiguous and recalcitrant to comprehension by category.

On the empirical side psychology participates in aesthetics because all aesthetic objects have to reduce to the experience that discovers them, while taste reduces to something in the mind that expresses it. In an empirical dimension, then, "the subject matter of aesthetics, however various, may be swallowed up in the psychological vortex, together with everything else that exists."[77] But, assuming the province of psychology to be limited to human experience, some things are able to transcend it. Mathematics, history, and the judgments following from taste do not entail psychology, other than "adventitiously and for a third person." Psychological categories may subsume the whole universe and still there would be a remainder constituted by every human pursuit, every field of experience, and every faith in its respective hypostasis. The paradox of aesthetics is that "aesthetic experience will continue to elude and overflow psychology in a hundred ways although in its own way psychology might eventually survey and represent all aesthetic experience."[78]

Whereas Santayana assigns aesthetic facts to psychology as one species of the various presentations it interprets, he assigns aesthetic values to moral philosophy as one among other species of ethical data it idealizes. Moral dialectic, or moral idealism, starts with the organism's animal will. From this non-cognitive source, with the assistance of the rational principle of harmony and equilibrium, it develops ideals, thereby differentiating itself from mathematical dialectic which starts from simple intuitions[79] and, with the assistance of deduction, develops tautologies. It is moral idealism that has most to do with aesthetics on the rational side. The moral ideal involved presupposes an antecedent and a consequent. The antecedent is irrational. It is the impulse to embody some latent tendency in an explicit form.[80] But there is a condition attached to this project. To succeed it must accommodate itself to all other interests of the artist. Granting this adjustment as achieved, the non-artistic interests will merge to support the one toward art, that is, will function to assist in its fulfillment.[81] The consequent, too, is irrational. It consists of the satisfaction from the completed work. This satisfaction, in turn, becomes one ingredient in the individual artist's happiness. Thus the rational element in Santayana's moral philosophy of aesthetic activity lies in a field between two irrational poles: the original impulse and the final satisfaction. Yet neither the first nor the last stage is possible without the ideal and the fact of harmony in the reason and conative organization respectively, of the individual acting as an artist. An aesthetic good never is a separate thing but always is intertwined both with the vital processes and the moral idealism of some individual.[82] Since the ideal varies with the individual, Santayana is maintaining his customary relative pluralism. Throughout the construction of the aesthetic object imagination will be used, but reason stands guard over this faculty to guarantee the tempering of all the imaginative parts of the organism's behavior and thus prepare them for harmony with all other parts.[83] This kind of control conforms, in a thoroughly classical fashion, to the objective of avoiding strife or collapse and preserving concord and equilibrium.

Under the terms of his analysis Santayana decides that aesthetics is neither part of psychology nor of philosophy and further that neither the history of man nor of art "isolate any such block of experience as aesthetics is supposed to describe."[84]

Aesthetics is estranged from a distinctive correspondence with some unique region of human experience, and any attempt to find such correspondence will be futile. In the ideal region, however, a more favorable condition prevails. While in the ideal region a complete unadulterated aesthetic science is not conceivable, there nevertheless is a respectable substitute found in the art and function of criticism. Criticism is "a reasoned appreciation of human works" and it presupposes "a mind not wholly ignorant of their subject, their occasion, their school, and their process of manufacture."[85] Here Santayana's view embraces all criticism and is not in the least restricted to the fine arts. Criticism further has a locus within certain categories of reference it employs when judging any work. These categories are: beauty, propriety, difficulty, originality, truth, and moral significance.

The moral philosopher also has a place in criticism. His function is to combine into a harmonious ideal all the points brought out by the categories used in critical appraisal. By this means a standard for relative estimation of the technical products is established and this standard must have the additional property of being a goal influencing human effort.[86] Thus in respect to criticism Santayana is both normative and naturalistically teleological. This rational composition of a standard of aesthetic criticism must embody, besides "the interest and delight which men find in something beautiful," other interests of the individual.[87] Moreover, the two kinds of interests— aesthetic and non-aesthetic—must form a harmonious balance with each other. In Santayana's view to abstract an aesthetic interest from harmonious integration with others and make this one interest unique and self-sufficient is to act outside of a moral milieu.[88] His kind of aesthetics is rational, contextualistic, pluralistic, and relativistic. It is contemptible to honor a solitary aesthetic sphere, but what is even worse is the irrational state of moral anarchy that an isolated aesthetics inaugurates. The removal of the aesthetic force or support from the equilibrium maintained within the rational ideal precipitates the collapse of the whole structure. With the one buttress withdrawn, the others disperse, and the outcome is diverse units scattered in irrationality. The debacle transforms to chaos what had been a cosmos.[89] A self-contained aesthetics is a fantastic abstraction, comparable to a mathematics without application or a morality without reference to life.

Santayana offers still other objections to the excision of aesthetics, one of which is curious. He suggests that, man's nature and expressions in living being what they are, it would not be possible to divorce the aesthetic element completely and finally from them. His supposition regarding what would happen is that, after the aesthetic ingredient was withdrawn, the remainder, or supposed non-aesthetic portion, would soon begin to reveal to man something that would arouse the value of beauty.[90] Santayana is convinced that something in man and his relation to the outside world forbids that beauty is expugnable. The attempt to isolate an aesthetic factor invites a never-ending regression: each time the aesthetic part is separated, the assumed non-aesthetic remainder develops an aesthetic character to nullify what has been done.[91] The human eye, confronted solely with an environment of things customarily dismissed as non-aesthetic, tends to make an aesthetic adjustment to the practical objects among them. It begins to trace forms in things it otherwise would have ignored and these forms stimulate a reaction of beauty, thereby restoring aesthetic experience to the organism.[92] In other words, the relation of man and his environment is incorrigibly aesthetic, and, no matter what is taken away, the value of beauty will arise out of psychological transactions with the remainder.

Santayana's concluding observation in "What Is Aesthetics?" is that the value of beauty is inextricably associated with other values: they would remain incomplete, therefore imperfect, "if beauty did not supervene upon them; beauty would be impossible if they did not underlie it."[93] Among all values there must be respective interdependence in order to maintain the integrity of each. Santayana maintains that there can be no such thing as a pleasure of perception not merged in a unity with something in the moral as well as in the natural world.[94] His theory demands a state of continuity between things empirical and things rational. If pleasure of perception inevitably is in continuous relation with all other values, that is, with all other good, then the presence of pleasantness may be interpreted as "a symbol of total excellence." At the same time "knowledge of what things are, of what skill means, of what man has endured and desired, re-enters like a flood that no man's land of mere aestheticism."[95] This is the assumption that Santayana elaborates in *The Life of Reason*.

7. Poetry and Philosophy

The remaining work among the major monuments of Santayana's treatment of criticism is the volume of six lectures based on a course he had given at Harvard from 1907 to 1910 and titled *Three Philosophical Poets*. The contents of this work are more a practical illustration of the principles determining Santayana's highest level of poetry than a presentation of critical theory. The lectures reveal no new principles, nor do they alter in the least the theory of the highest level which requires rational presentation of subject matter of the widest scope. As mentioned in *Interpretations of Poetry and Religion* a prominent feature of this level is that on it poetry and religion come to be identical kinds of expression. In the viewpoint contained in *Three Philosophical Poets* it is poetry and philosophy that seem to merge, and Santayana provides an account of this relationship.

The general bearing of *Three Philosophical Poets* is more toward philosophy than toward poetry, however, although in parts of the exposition there are passages having definite significance for the field of aesthetic criticism. The chief question raised within critical theory concerns the interrelation of poetry and philosophy, but the implications of this question bring forward several interesting topics, including brevity in poetic presentation, the potential of philosophy as a source of inspiration, the emotional metaphysics of philosophical poetry, the unity of value and the plurality of facts, symbolic priority as between things and ideas, congruence of the poetic accomplishment and the moral life, philosophical theory as poetic content, and finally, diversity in modes of art.

The examples of Lucretius, Dante, and Goethe form an excellent setting in which to ask questions about the theoretical propriety of conjoining philosophy and poetry. Each was an eminent poet, and each represented a different philosophy. Lucretius exhibits a thoroughgoing naturalism that includes in one complete system both materialism in natural science and humanism in ethics. Dante avers supernaturalism. His subject matter is of the widest comprehension since it embraces all of heaven, all of earth, and all of the individuals in both seen under the form of a rational philosophical organization. Goethe is the poet of romanticism and is akin in viewpoint to philosophers who place "a mystical faith in will and action." On the basis of this evidence Santayana asks the axial questions of his lectures: "Are poets, at heart, in search of a philosophy? Or is philosophy, in the end, nothing but poetry?"[96]

Santayana begins the construction of his answers to the questions he has asked by pointing out a common ground on which to identify, at least partially, poetry and philosophy. In *Interpretations of Poetry and Religion* he had used a similar method in stating that the imagination was the single agent productive of the "large ideas" of poetry, religion, and philosophy.[97] In *Three Philosophical Poets* there is little variation of this approach. Instead of mentioning the common ground or unifying agent as the psychological faculty of imagination, he calls this common basis "vision," a term suited to the philosophical context in which he finds himself. He prefaces his assertion of vision by a discrimination within philosophical thinking itself. Philosophy "as an investigation into truth or as reasoning upon truths supposed to be discovered" will result in nothing "akin to poetry."[98] But besides the activity of non-poetical reasoning, there is in philosophy an activity of vision.[99]

It is in the order of vision that philosophy and poetry meet. Reasoned investigation keeps the two disintegrated, but vision lets them coalesce. Withal, reasoning and investigation are not irrelevant to vision but continuous with it. They are preliminary stages, of a seemingly servile kind, that in their culmination reach the threshold of vision.[100] It is in the state of vision or contemplation that the philosopher and the poet momentarily may interchange their identities.[101] But apart from this apex where a symmetrical relation is more or less spontaneously achieved, it is easier for the philosopher to be a poet than for the poet to be a philosopher. Something about the character of each of the respective pursuits aids or handicaps the individual representative of each in his effort to become a representative of the other. Philosophy in its own character tends to be "reasoned and heavy," while poetry tends to be "winged, flashing, inspired." The philosopher in his best moments may become a poet, but the poet will be in his worst moments if he succeeds in becoming a philosopher.

The context of the poet and the philosopher affords Santayana an opportunity to make a transition to the field of literary criticism. If he is going to claim that the poet and the philosopher may interchange functions, then he must be ready for the objection based on the evidence that poetic expression may be extremely brief, whereas philosophical expression includes conceptual developments that require it to be of some length. In other words, it appears as if the mere physical state of composition, that is, the comparative number of sound images used, were going to be a barrier to any merger of poetry and philosophy. Also, the sustained character of the long poem inevitably precludes a uniformly high quality throughout and, in any long poem, a part will be better than the rest or than the whole, a condition which further strengthens the case of the advocate that one criterion of the best poetry is brevity.

Santayana has chosen Lucretius, Dante, and Goethe as his supreme poets, and if it is the rapturous mood of the fleeting moment or the quickly depicted episode that is of the essence of poetry, then his critical project is a failure. Santayana anticipates this hazard and meets it in a discussion of two types of poets that he plainly and picturesquely designates as "long-winded" and "short-winded." As he presents the issue it centers around the question: are we "better poets in a line than in an epic"?[102] He begins the defense of his own persuasion by submitting examples of the short-winded poet and some ordinary unimaginative person in the state of either talking or staring. Both these examples may be seen under the category of experiences of a moment. So in some respects the experiences are the same. As far as the act of bare thinking is concerned the non-poetic person is on a par with the poet. It remains to point out the principal difference between the two, which is that the poet excels the non-poet, not in thinking but in feeling.[103] Each of the two experiences is only a moment but the poet's moment "has a vision, a scope, a symbolic something about it that renders it deep and expressive."[104] The difference between a moment of poetic insight and a vulgar moment is that "the passions of the poetic moment have more perspective."[105] The poet is thus discriminated from the ordinary man but not yet shown to be in kind with the philosopher. It is with the assistance of diction that the broad perspective attributed to the passions of the poet approaches philosophy. The words selected by the poet "have a magic momentum in them which carries us, we know not how, to mountain tops of intuition."[106] By possessing a broad perspective of feeling plus the capacity to attain a peak on the intuitive level of man's thought the poet, independently of any linear measurement of his product, has practically become a philosopher.[107]

Poetic brevity, then, has been shown to be no insurmountable obstacle to philosophy, and those who would exclude poetry from philosophy on the basis of verbal magnitude have been answered. However, Santayana still has to reveal how a long poem can be more effective philosophically than a short one. He does this by recourse to a consideration of the variation between the long and the short poem in respect to capacity for suggestion. He assumes that a short passage of poetry can be pregnant with suggestion of only a few things and states the rhetorical question: "How much more poetical ought a vision to be which was pregnant with all we care for?"[108] The obvious answer implied is taken to support the position he affirms. He next moves nearer to the desired conclusion by considering the act of focusing experience. A small portion of experience focused in the poetic moment was asserted to have scope and depth of feeling and at the same time to be of imaginative substance. Santayana now requests the performance of a thought experiment with the conditions that the feeling of the poetic moment be given more scope and more depth, so that *all* of experience is focused within it. With these conditions satisfied Santayana believes there is a state reached wherein philosophy and poetry may be identified. A view of all of experience assumed in the expanded poetic moment which will represent the long poem corresponds to a philosopher's vision of the world.[109] In turn, the philosopher by the activity of his own vision within his own province "will grow imaginative in a superlative degree, and be supremely poetical."[110] It seems that Santayana makes the difference between poetry and philosophy one of degree and not of kind. It requires the long poem to gain the fullest coincidence with philosophy, and the scope the long poem may achieve gives it a poetic merit denied to a short poem.[111] The true comparison of a long and a short poem is not by number of lines but by the range of imaginative experience.[112] It is the experience of a vision that is decisive, the verbal expression of the vision being mainly the instrument that suspends the experience in thought so that "others may be able to decipher it, and to be stirred by it as by a wind of suggestion sweeping the whole forest of their memories."[113]

But philosophy has other relations to poetry than simply that of mere duplication of vista. Philosophy, especially naturalistic philosophy, may be a source of poetic inspiration.[114] Naturalism may direct the poet to incorporate serious import in his product and turn his attention from the sterile distraction of his own will to a spring of creativity in the imagination.[115] Yet perhaps the most valuable of all the kinds of inspiration emerging from naturalistic philosophy is its stimulation of the poet's emotions. In this influence the texture of poetry is being created.[116]

Regarding the question of philosophy and emotion Santayana has further comments that are rather penetrating in character. He suggests that the emotion apparently associated with some wide philosophical doctrine is really associated with a presentation of life, because a different body of doctrine covering the same scope will arouse the same emotion as the doctrine it replaces.[117] Moreover, whatever the variation in the conceptual formulation of the universe may be, assuming the formulation to be comprehensive and mature, the values that respond to it will be constant. Santayana's conviction is that any adequate presentation of life in its widest purview gives rise to one and the same emotion[118] and hence to one and the same value regardless of the terms in which the presentation is couched.[119] The corollary of this standpoint is equally profound. It consists of Santayana's decision that non-discursive symbols, apprehended non-cognitively, constitute the medium of philosophical contact with reality.[120] In matters of universal scope neither enumeration nor rationally formulated relations of a pluralism of facts is able to supersede a monism of value.

Preparatory to a statement about moral affairs and philosophical poetry Santayana inserts an observation about the philosophical poet's treatment of symbols. For the philosophical poet the ordinary habit of construing a word as a symbol is minimized and emphasis is placed instead on things as symbols of ideals:[121] it is an ideal that is the thing symbolized and its symbol is other things. The ideal symbolized, then, may be a moral ideal and poetry can embrace content which is the setting for a moral life. The best example of poetry so disposed is that of Dante.[122]

By incorporating philosophy in the form of poetry Santayana realizes he is inviting various objections. Ordinarily theory itself is not considered as being of an aesthetic nature and accordingly is not in place in such an aesthetic expression as poetry. Historically any literary form embodying didacticism has not achieved a high rank. Also theory within poetry suggests misplacement of function and other incongruities. Santayana is conscious of these associations and sees that he must provide an explanation that will forestall a derogatory misinterpretation of his principles. He clarifies his position by pointing out that poetry and theory, in his use of the terms, are not two things but one. Therefore the presence of theory in poetry is not objectionable but is fitting and commendable.[123] Poetry's highest attainment is the exhibition of the organization of all things as a value occurring in the imagination, and this is the manner in which theory belongs in poetry.[124] Poetry falling short of this terminus is correspondingly minor poetry.

One final theoretical statement in *Three Philosophical Poets* concerns the integration of poetry with that large conception which Santayana denotes as rational art and which is explicated so extensively in *The Life of Reason*. Poetry that would stand as art in isolation must be eschewed. In such a position poetry would, in effect, deny the entire concept of rational art. Poetry cannot be allowed to have its exclusive domain, for rational art demands a harmonious organization of all arts. However Santayana readily recognizes that one art, while continuous with another, is not interchangeable with it.

The condition of diversity among component arts within rational art permits an analysis whereby rational art may be seen to contain two modes. One of these is found in association with the instrumental pursuits which adjust us to our environment, for example, industry, science, and morality. In these activities the actual conduct of life may be carried on "joyfully, artistically, and sympathetically" to render them a mode of art.[125] The other mode is art as it would express the moral ideal toward which we move by reason of the conditions achieved by our practical conduct. The first mode, then, is for the sake of the second; in other words, "the outer life is for the sake of the inner, the discipline is for the sake of the freedom, and conquest for the sake of self-possession."[126] We live and know in our environment according to how we progress in the first sort of art, yet it is the second sort of art—the projection and enjoyment of an ideal—that gives direction to the first.[127] It is by thus interacting in a continuous unity that the two modes functionally are always one rational art.[128]

To summarize, Santayana's main doctrines of poetry and its criticism fall under three aspects: first, a foundation in a psychology, whereby understanding is akin to imagination; second, a claim of actual identity between poetry and religion; and third, an assertion of a scale for comparing poetic accomplishment. Understanding is a species of imagination and continuous with it; both are prophecy. Prophecies of the understanding are verifiable within the operation of sense perception and may warrant success in practical action; prophecies of imagination are not verifiable in sense perception and carry no warrant of success in practical action. In the dimension of an imaginative construction poetry and religion are identical, although nominally they are distinguishable. The name, religion, is assigned when the construction intervenes in the conduct of life. The name, poetry, is assigned when the construction merely supervenes on life. At the point of utmost development of each, they are indistinguishable. Poetry attains its highest rank when it is moral in character, cosmic in scope and profound in insight. On its lowest level poetry is principally sensuous. Between the two it is romantic in type. But on every level the source of poetry is emotional experience. All poetry is an interaction of something rational and something irrational. The irrational emotional factor unifies the poetic elements, according to a principle of beauty; the rational factor provides an order for these same elements and points to a moral objective.

Santayana's earliest search for principles of criticism was inconclusive and merely indicated awareness of diverse points of view with regard to the language, interpretation, and moral consequences of poetry, as well as with regard to the place of convention, illusion, communication, and feeling in the poetic product. Continued attention to criticism led him to explore the significance of the term, aesthetics. It is found equivocal in three respects: first, it fails to designate activity exclusively physical or exclusively of thought; second, it fails to demarcate itself as exclusively within the scope of psychology or exclusively outside of it; third, it fails to be concerned exclusively with fact or exclusively with value. It cannot be interpreted in isolation but is rational, contextualistic, and relativistic; moreover, man inevitably has an aesthetic relation to his environment.

A later concept parallels the identity of poetry and religion with an identity of poetry and philosophy, exhibited by Lucretius, Dante, and Goethe. Lucretius represents an identity of poetry and naturalism, Dante of poetry and supernaturalism, and Goethe of poetry and romanticism. In the state of philosophic contemplation the poet and the philosopher are indistinguishable. They both possess one broad perspective of feeling and both reach one high intuitive level, making superficial distinctions between them disappear. Life, when presented as naturalistic, gives rise to a single emotion, regardless of any variation of terms in which this emotion is represented. Philosophy and the greatest poetry are equally theoretical insofar as both depict an organization of things as a value occurring in imagination; while in the dimension of reason each integrates with the other to support a moral idea.

CHAPTER IV

Rational Art

■

1. *The Rational Ideal*

In Santayana's views of man's aesthetic domain there are three main centers of emphasis: first, the individual's aesthetic experience in itself; second, the criticism that may be applied to the aesthetic product as found in poetry; and third, the participation of the aesthetic factor as it meshes with reason to become an ingredient in man's program and conduct of life or, as Santayana would say, in man's moral life. These three aspects are usually present when Santayana treats aesthetic subject matter even though one of them may be amplified while the other two are subdued.

Prior to 1905 Santayana had emphasized in turn the aesthetic experience, poetry, and criticism. He restricted the aesthetic experience to the subjective functioning that elicits from the organism the value of beauty and stressed the biological sources of the sensuous side of aesthetics. He followed this account with an exposition of the critical faculty of man as it may formulate canons when human judgment is exercised in the presence of an art product and poetry is the art product being judged. In 1905 he moved the third and most comprehensive part of his doctrine to the center of the stage. It is in this part that the juncture of art and all of human living is emphasized; that the vital interaction of man and his world is examined; that the human powers to idealize through reason are stressed; and that the question is asked, what is the place of art in all experience?

In the first presentation of his thinking in aesthetics Santayana was mainly in the field of psychology; in the second he was in the field of art criticism; in the third he is in the field of ethics. It is within this third background that he conducts his most complete examination of art products and his views are summarized in *Reason in Art* which appeared in 1905 as the fourth volume of a five-volume work titled *The Life of Reason or the Phases of Human Progress*, published over the two-year period 1905–1906. This work was by no means the first indication of the conceptions it contains. There had been intermittent reference to the same conceptions for at least ten years before they were developed to book length.[1] *The Life of Reason* is merely the fullest statement of them, not the first. Santayana constantly seems to have been inclined to study the interaction of man and environment as recorded by the existence of art, and to deal with this question insofar as it included all environmental factors and not merely those classed as aesthetic. Whatever that environment may be—economic, political, religious, or something else—Santayana sought to reveal wherein it participated in some art process and wherein it did not. He looked for the effects of the individual man's artlike activities upon his environment as well as the effects of the environment upon the individual practicing art.

The nucleus for Santayana's thought about man and man's environment is a concept he calls the Life of Reason,[2] a pervasive doctrine that implies considerable reflection on the topic of art. Moreover, the doctrine treats art quite directly through the circumstance that the Life of Reason presupposes a harmonious combination of diverse ideal elements subsumed within three main classifications of human activity, one of which is art itself; the others are science and religion.[3] Each of these three types of activity conjoins the others in the Life of Reason, but each remains in a position subordinate to the total rational harmony they comprise and in which they are continuous and complementary to each other. In this context art is ancillary only to reason, and aesthetic theory founded on the presupposed context is characterized by being both rational and functional.

The Life of Reason is Santayana's label for an old Hellenic doctrine founded by Socrates,[4] glorified by Plato,[5] and sobered and solidified by Aristotle.[6] In Santayana's version this doctrine incorporates three basic theories. Of these, two are ancient and the third is modern. The first of the ancient theories is that harmony and equilibrium of both body and soul are equivalent to a good, as advocated by the Pythagoreans and as formulated later in the "mean" of Aristotle; the second is almost exclusively associated with Aristotle, being that "everything ideal has a natural basis and everything natural an ideal development."[7] The modern influence is the belief in progress as stressed by nineteenth-century theories of biological and other forms of evolution.[8]

Looking at man in a state prior to the Life of Reason, Santayana finds a biological organism with certain physiological and psychological equipment. Man, in the course of his living experience, may use this equipment for or against himself. Its main divisions are two processes: that of impulse and that of ideation.[9] If man allows his impulse free rein and suppresses his ideation, he tends to become a brute; if he suppresses his impulse and allows his ideation full sway he tends to become a maniac. Clearly both of these excesses call for tempering. By uniting the two processes so that something like an Aristotelian mean accrues, Santayana finds the key to what permits man to be designated as a "rational animal."[10] The balanced integration of the two factors will give man ideas applicable to his environment and at the same time conduce to actions that have beneficial consequence and may be classified as morally good. Under these conditions man natively has at his disposal the capacity both to improve his own life and to contribute generically to human progress. Santayana is assuming that man, in his given animal state, has a propulsive energy and also has imagination; and that whatever he finds propitious in his endeavors he will call good and whatever he finds hostile to them he will call evil.[11]

The whole doctrine shrouds three fundamental implications: first, that within the order of his own nature there is available to man a rational morality; second, that man's life as progressive may be seen as a drama; and third, that progress is within the limitations of human acts. The view of progress is interlocked with that of life as a drama, for progress itself is conceived as the kind of action that occurs to give life the aspect of a drama.[12] Man primitively has the capacity to reflect and to represent ideal goals to himself. He has also the faculty of memory. These abilities enable him to look forward and backward, to recall what is absent, and to project what sometime may be present, and, in an affective dimension to be subject to regret and to desire; while concurrent with these affective and ideational states, man is permeated with sensations. As soon as the flux of sensations is transcended, he is able to reflect and to engage in representation which in turn may assume any of three modes: it may be idle; or speculative; or programmatic.[13] But of these only programmatic representation is of concern to Santayana. In this kind of representation man endeavors to use his power of reflection as an aid toward modifying his future.[14] Out of reflection a program arises carrying the expectation that, at some future time, some sort of realization of the program will have taken place. When the appointed time has come and if the modification that was in prospect has been accomplished, it may be said, according to Santayana's doctrine, that man has exercised his reason.

Automatically accompanying this representative and rational activity of man is the presence of a value. The activity includes the distinctive circumstance of imputing a value where the value cannot yet be felt. When reflection collects the experiences that are the elements from which to make the future modification, an act of comparison between the present and the projected states is involved and a relative value is bound to arise.[15] The function of modifying the individual's environment will then embody two interests: one ideal and for the future, and one definitely a condition that is present. The rational life will attend to the present state and simultaneously maintain an interest in the ideal future harmony; under these conditions life itself may be designated as "reason in operation."

One more major characteristic of the Life of Reason is that it constantly upholds a state of happiness as its goal. Reason, solely by the condition of being reason, always will aim to generate or augment happiness, and, to this end, will exert control on conduct. Underlying Santayana's view of the rational ideal is a recognition of hedonism. On the level of sense, pleasure is assumed to be good and pain to be evil.[16] Yet, while sense pleasure may be a good, it has limitations: there is no human progress to be achieved from the instrumentality of sense pleasure alone. Santayana will not allow sense by itself to determine an individual's progress. In progress there must be a moral life served by the conjunction of reflection and the formulated ideal whose realization signifies progress.[17] There is in the Life of Reason provision for pleasures of sense, but they are included only to the extent that they are part of a rational program guiding conduct toward an ideal goal, characterized by being a harmony of instincts or vital impulses.[18]

A striking feature of the Life of Reason is the way in which its character seems to coincide with the character of art, in the widest sense of that term.[19] The likeness suggested persists over several aspects of both terms and invites the opinion that the Life of Reason is art in both practice and principle. Each element one would discover in some given work of art seems to have its homologue in Santayana's Life of Reason. A work of art arises from a human operation. So does the Life of Reason. Art is identified with a purpose consciously guiding this operation. So is the Life of Reason. The method or technique that constructs the art product is teachable. So is the method of the Life of Reason. This embodiment of purpose and existence of communicable technique are elements that transform desultory human operations into an art.[20]

There are further correspondences. Like the Life of Reason, art embodies a creative idea, and the art product when analyzed will exhibit each part discretely as a rational ingredient which combined into a whole realizes a distinctively pleasing concretion of the original idea. Moreover, both art and the Life of Reason are results of a prior method and situation rather than detached powers in themselves. They again have similar requirements for being instituted: liberal genius and a favorably plastic environment.[21] It is noteworthy and fundamental that both art and reason arise from natural sources and use natural material. Likewise they both elevate a given and fairly indeterminable process or operation to a higher and definitely rational stage, and the outcome must always have moral value. The ideas involved in art and the Life of Reason must be practical; otherwise neither would come to be.[22] A central observation concerning reflection and its consequences as displayed in both art and the Life of Reason is that these endeavors emphatically establish that the natural world is a fitting and beneficial home for the human individual.

However, Santayana warns against the inference that nature is always and everywhere plastic in the face of art and reason.[23] He develops the point by considering an extrapolation in which art would be expanded to a magnitude embracing every activity in nature. Thereby all nature would exist as amenable to art and, under that condition, reason would be a ubiquitous first principle. Such a grandiose conception would amount to a confusion of function and cause.[24] To have reason coextensive with nature and effective over nature's vast domain is to overlook facts which may affirm that all activities of nature may not be commensurable with reason. Santayana concludes that the universalizing of reason in nature is a speculative fable, or a poetic expression of an ideal. Nevertheless for most individuals every ideal has a natural basis, definable in these elected instances,[25] even though not in the mass total of all human beings and over all of nature. It is likewise a truism that any ideal is a natural goal originating from an impulse.[26]

2. *Art and Human Nature*

Art, as a natural activity of man, reverts for its most remote antecedents to two factors: an organism and an environment, with each given as possessing the property of plasticity.[27] These serve as a primitive premise from which Santayana draws an elaborate pattern of inferences, with the assistance of the corollary that there is interaction between the organism and its environment. Here Santayana indicates complete acceptance of Herbert Spencer's once popular declaration that "life is the continuous adjustment of internal relations to external relations."[28]

One of the immediate implications of these primitive terms is that there is a two-way flow of action between any organism and its environment, with a twofold result with respect to the organism: it will not only impress itself on the environment but also will be impressed by the environment.[29] Of these two results only the flow from the organism to its environment pertains to art.[30]

In the impress that the organism makes on its environment there is, within each term, a specific constituent which is primary to the transaction. In the case of the organism that constituent is instinct; in the case of the environment it is the material given in the real object.[31] Instinct and material are the bare components out of which art develops, but although necessary for this development they are not sufficient to assure it. The interaction of the organism's impulse and the environmental material will leave a product, but that product may belong in either of two categories: it may have utility or it may not. If it does not have utility it is disqualified from classification as art; if it has utility it is eligible to become art. The product will assume the full status of art when it meets the further condition that the impressing organism, in other words the maker or doer, is at times conscious of the utility of what he is doing. If the maker or doer is sometimes conscious of the utility of what he is doing, the product is art;[32] if he is completely unaware of utility in his product, even though it has potential utility, the product is not art.

Art, then, involves the action of an organism upon its environment leading to a result recognized by the organism as useful. Along with this event there is one important qualification being assumed as satisfied, namely that the procedure followed in the art may be transmitted to others,[33] and that others possess the aptitude for carrying out the procedure. Fortunately that qualification is covered by two attributes native to the organism, one being the capacity to teach and to be taught and the other being the capacity for imitation. Given an environment plastic to the organism, plus the tools of teaching and imitation to permit repetition of useful stampings on the environment, art, as Santayana sees it, is ready to establish itself as a natural and human institution. Neither outward necessity nor the presence of a worthy idea governs action toward art. Necessity, considered externally, is not the mother of invention, and ideas are not the motive power of art.[34] It is primarily human craving that generates art in man. To be sure, Santayana affirms that both an incipient pleasure and the recognition of some palpable objective must accompany the non-cognitive stimulus;[35] but without the conative dimension of the organism art would be without a point of origin and presumably man would be without art.

However important instinct may be in the origin of art, there is the equally important condition that art never remains confined by instinct, but soon breaks away from this inner source to become an outward product and, in the movement outward, reason is a guiding light.[36] The direction of the organism's movement as found in art is from an inward state to an outward form, not the reverse.[37] It is a movement with its aim controlled by the presence of reason and it ends in a material product.

Another fundamental relation within art is that between utility and structure. One of the attributes of art is acknowledged utility; but unless this utility can be conveyed to carry on progress, the art product is nullified. In this impasse, structure becomes of vast consequence, for through its instrumentality innumerable repetitions of the art act may be assured[38] and artists may continue in their ways. The structure of an art product has two roots: one in the artificer and another in the material he impresses. In the artificer structure is the basis of skill and perseverance; in the art material structure implies plasticity to the active skill.[39]

It is further required that all art have a rational end. The initial urge of the organism feels this end, which appears as some ideal goal that represents a good and guarantees happiness as a by-product. Santayana speaks literally when he calls the structure in art which assists reason "a happy organization."[40] There is a second by-product of art seen as a consequence of the force through which it acts on the totality of man's environment. Not quickly, but slowly and relentlessly, the continuous impression of the environment by the organism registers a change in the environment. It is to the very activity of art and the changes wrought by the expression of man's mind on matter that progress may be traced.[41] This inevitable provision for progress is the second by-product of art.

If man's welfare is contingent on changes in his environment, then man's welfare is contingent on the art of the past that has presented him with these changes.[42] It is also the case that the art of the future takes as its point of departure the environment given to it by the art of the past, which is to say that the art of the future is continuously interacting with the art of the past.[43] One result of this interaction is that man's power over his environment is perpetually accumulating. Assuming that power over environment assures improvement in the lot of man, then one consequence of art will be the satisfactions it offers mankind.[44] But art is even more than an environmental ladder to human amelioration. It is a preserver and carrier of rationality over future generations, an action salutary to the soul,[45] and by its own terms moves toward ideals whose attainment advances human interests physically, cognitively, and affectively, and thereby it has a place in the Life of Reason.[46]

3. Art and the Fine Arts

It is clear that in Santayana's usage art is a term of much wider comprehension than fine art, and that again he is following the Greeks who had distinguished *techne* (art) and *mimesis* (imitation). And it is also clear that in Santayana's view fine art sometimes lies outside the domain of art and, judged by the standards of the Life of Reason, commands no great respect.[47] One of the premises from which Santayana depreciates fine art supposes that the value from fine art centers in the imagination to a greater degree than in either sense or intelligence. The kind of value associated with the imagination is classified as predominantly an aesthetic value, being also called beauty. This value may occur in the presence of both art and nature.[48] When the occurrence is with reference to an art object, the given object usually will be denoted fine art. But it must be recalled that fine art, as commonly considered, entails an abstraction from some real object.[49] For Santayana the abstraction made in the conception of fine art is a false step because it rejects any utilitarian and moral value of the object from which the abstraction is made. Utilitarian and moral value cannot accompany an abstraction; they must remain attached to the real object.[50] But it is utilitarian and moral values that are required for the Life of Reason and if concern with fine art slights these values, then fine art must prepare to be slighted. Fundamentally, fine art, regardless of its conjunction with the value of beauty, is not thoroughly acceptable in the Life of Reason, although it is not objectionable as an accompaniment of it.[51]

Having a location mainly within imagination is not the only mark distinguishing fine art from art. There is another criterion founded on one of the organism's behavior states, designated as spontaneity or automatism. Each of these terms refers to the same initial phase of organic action that may be seen as a starting point yielding a work of art. Before discriminating fine art it is necessary to consider the genesis of art itself under the terms proposed. Spontaneous action, in the course of time, may build up some useful results which are taken as a basis to institute practices having recognized utility. Out of this kind of happening art grows.[52] Moreover, the spontaneous action which was a source of utility also may have a rational function, and when it has, it leads to art.[53]

With the objective of demarcating a region for the location of art Santayana conceives the extremes of spontaneity on the side of origin and utility on the side of practice. If given either spontaneity or utility in a pure state there is no art,[54] but either may be an influential factor leading to the development of art.[55] The art may be servile or liberal: servile if, like war, the basis for it is "some failure in politics and morals";[56] liberal, if fit material is appropriated for ideal uses such as in the fine arts of music and eloquence that may arise out of war.

Santayana now has a basis on which to differentiate the fine arts. They may come into being with the antecedents either of utility or of automatism. They contain something of each and in a perfect example would be completely expressive of both.[57] In such an example the utility never would have the character of practical compulsion and the creative impulse never would be irrelevant to progress.[58] But since human nature interacting with its environment is not a rationally perfect event, there is some need to compromise on the question of art, and, allowing for things as they are, the arts nearest either the extreme of automatism or the extreme of utility are the meanest arts, while those that are an admixture of automatism and utility are nobler.[59]

Historically, art as spontaneous precedes art as useful; also before the products of spontaneity can develop to products of utility and begin to function rationally, there must be considerable irresponsibility dissipated,[60] of which the dances, shouts, and other manifestations of ceremonies expressing the mythology of savages would be an example. Nevertheless the automatism of grimaces and gestures found in the savage's ceremony contains the seeds of art. The barbaric acts do strike an outer world or actual external situation, and somehow this environment functions as a corrective of their irresponsibility or purely automatic character. The modification of the acts by the discipline of environment brings some of them to the point[61] of having the utility and rationality that permit the emergence of art. Besides sheer utility and rationality in the product there are other results of the art-generating process. The primitive performer himself undergoes a transmutation. His own interaction with the disciplining world impresses certain restrictions on him and these enable him to become what may be called an artist and to develop elements of order and pleasant efficacy in his work that come to be denoted as his style.[62]

Generally speaking Santayana uses two criteria to discriminate the useful or rational arts from the fine arts. The first criterion is utility itself; the second is the principle of rational integration. The two overlap by mutual implication. For the most part fine arts are excluded by both. Fine arts are of neither immediate nor proximate use and are alien to combination with other acts or expressions of the human individual bent upon setting up a practical ideal. Fine arts are not art in the best sense, for in the best sense art is an element in a rational program, a position denied to most works of fine art. They are more like an inexpugnable element accompanying art.[63] They may be decorative; they may arouse the value of beauty;

they may even partake of utility; but fine arts themselves are not useful, not rational, not conducive to human progress,[64] and not the stuff of human ideal goals.[65] Nevertheless in origins fine arts and rational or industrial arts are the same; either type will reduce to some automatism, that is, to the action of some physically organic process.[66]

Music may be seen to originate from the stimulus of sound,[67] which in turn depends on the acts of sound producing organs in man or animal species, given complementary impetus by the ear's ability to apprehend individual sounds and by the muscles of the body responding to rhythm.[68] Genetically music is a wail before it is a fine art. Poetry and other literature derive from language; and language has part of the same organic base as music: respiratory system and ear.[69] The spontaneous act of emitting language is originally permeated with emotion. Animal cries and human sighs are heralds of poetry.[70] It is the exercise of human organs engaging in automatic expression that is the basis of music, poetry, and prose.

Painting and sculpture demand a different conception to account for their foundation. They differ from music and poetry in origin chiefly by the kind of construction they involve. The variety of construction used in painting and sculpture leaves a mark on the organism's environment; the variety of construction used in music and poetry does not. This mark created by plastic construction is an evidence of the individual organism's will and remains palpable for some appreciable duration; while construction of the variety occurring in the origins of music and poetry is here and gone for it is merely an automatism or self-expression of an organ exercising itself. In contrast the act of the organism in plastic construction is voluntary. Its original state may be something like breaking a stick or piling a heap of sand. A further differentia of the construction used in painting and sculpture is that it gives a new form to some material in the same process that it makes something in the environment obey the organism's will and idea. In accordance with this treatment of environmental material, painting and sculpture are designated as plastic arts. Like all the other constructions of the organism, that which foretells painting and sculpture grows from a promise of art to full definition. The stage of art is reached when the change the organism makes in its environment is accompanied by the knowledge of ensuing benefits. In other words, when plastic construction obeys reason plastic impulse becomes art.[71] The resulting art may include an aesthetic constituent arising from some aesthetic quality contributed by the agency of visual perception; for example, on the motivation associated with an aesthetic faculty, a savage may have twisted a flowering branch into the first wreath.[72] Both plastic art and plastic fine art develop in moments or stages. By rearranging chance arrangements of nature, man may gain a creative habit of introducing consonances into his surroundings, while subsequently he may transcend this gain through modification of the result by self-criticism.[73]

Architecture, too, is an outgrowth of plastic construction. Santayana perhaps considers architecture as the most worthy of the arts, for it is persistently a product derived from reason and useful to man. Architecture, by Santayana's criteria, would be the fine art par excellence because typically it is rational art in spite of other characteristics that permit it to be called fine art.

Two further means contribute largely to the advance from the stage of exercise of some of the body's organs to that of rational art and fine art. These means are structure and imitation. When the antecedent stages of music, literature, and architecture move to the verge of becoming arts, the principle of structure proves to be of great assistance to reason. Structure is the instrumentality of a rich versification in music, comparable to mathematics or arabesques;[74] and of the rhymes and rhythms that make memorable sensations for organizing and propagating poetry, even if these memorable sensations happen to be nonsense.[75] Judged by the category of structure, architecture is plainly foremost among the arts, for architecture is itself a self-sustaining structure, embodying beauty within its utility.[76] The fine arts of sculpture and painting use structure to some degree but not as directly as music, poetry, and architecture. Painting and sculpture are fundamentally imitative arts; they may leave their embryonic stage as a result of a series of random impressions on environmental material in imitation of things,[77] rather than with the assistance of structure. The elements of music and poetry, that is, musical sound and language, are not sensibly present in inorganic things. In contrast, the elements of sculpture and painting, that is, color, shape, and material, are present. Imitation, then, may be invoked to assist in constructing art products in the likeness of things, a representation of man like a man, and a representation of a landscape like a landscape. Not only does the principle of imitation assist reason as a force in the development of the arts, especially of painting and sculpture, but the same principle also is entirely congruent with the physiology of the organism. Images are involved in the act of imitation, and, physiologically, all images are motor.[78] Accordingly, in a physiological dimension, imitative art becomes continuous with sensation, so that Santayana calls imitation the fulfilment of a sensation,[79] rather than mere achievement of a similarity.[80] Both imitation and its congenial physiological supplement make an ideal representation easier than otherwise.

Structure and imitation, then, offer conspicuous assistance to the achievement of rationality, and rationality is achieved when the art product satisfies a purpose. This purpose, however, must meet two conditions: first, it must be warranted by its consistency with some ideal; and second, this ideal must be harmoniously adequate in the context of the producer's total or ultimate nature.[81] Santayana's views of art apply to the man ordinarily called an artisan to the same extent as to one called an artist; in fact, they often may apply more fully to an artisan. It is not how exceptional the artist is; what matters is the rationality of his art.

Since a man's actions viewed as repetitious mechanical procedure making an impression on his environment meet some of Santayana's requirements for art, he is impelled to face the question of how such action can conform with an ideal. He concludes that it can conform with the ideal of obtaining a result with a minimum of effort and that this result begets the further one of cheaper goods.[82] Furthermore, the combined results are equivalent to a restricted example of larger ideals of abundance in material products and reduction of toil to obtain the products.[83] However he does not admit that mere reduction of labor is itself moral and rational. The reduction is moral and rational only when it liberates energies to be expended in other fields and thereby increases the aggregate of items by which to calculate human accomplishment.[84] Santayana does not specify the other fields. He is emphasizing that all ideals must be interpreted, not prescribed. The instrumentality of mechanical operations does not generate rationality directly. The rationality occurs in a spiritual way, in a generation of some spiritual existence plus a valuation. Mechanical procedures are only adjuncts to this spiritual accomplishment.[85] This kind of spiritual constituent within rationality is presupposed as given within man.[86] Nevertheless the concept of a perpetually unembodied ideal or spiritual factor is not at all acceptable to Santayana. He insists on material representation of what the ideal is.[87] From the other side, action or thought without an ideal is nonsense.[88] The great distinction of art is that it is a medium through which man may transform the irrational material environment to a piece of evidence proclaiming the material formation of some rational ideal.[89]

To support his assertion of the several diverse factors affecting the art product, for example, mechanical labor, matter, form, reason, ideal, Santayana must grant that in the end art itself has two stages. One of these is mechanical or industrial, the other is liberal. The mechanical arts carry on a more direct struggle with the materials of nature than the liberal arts, which are concerned with a spirit of things. Mechanical arts also act as a necessary bridge between raw matter of nature and the same matter formed to accord with the ideal of man.[90] Santayana maintains there is continuity between the two stages of art. They are not discrete; they flow in an unbroken sequence and each has some character of the other,[91] while they consistently conspire to the same end.

The conspiracy of the mechanical arts and the liberal arts to remodel nature by reason seems, in Santayana's doctrine, almost to reject fine art as a serious factor in the life of man.[92] In this position he seems to be echoing the political thinking of Plato's *Republic* with its prescriptions and proscriptions in matters of art. Yet he is not literally accepting the orthodox interpretation of Plato's proclamations. He would rather see the strictures in the *Republic* as a tribute to art,[93] suggesting that he recognizes some similarity to his own views and wants to avert association of them with a puritanical condemnation of aesthetic values.[94] However, he does not relax his austerity with respect to fine art. To be admitted to the domain of reason, fine art must qualify by the standards of reason[95] and not by the character of fine art.[96] It is human uses, not pleasure in and from creation, that give works of art their highest charm. It may be that fine art can be part of the Life of Reason, but, if so, it is included under restrictions, not through inevitability. Fine art may occasionally embrace some character that allows it to carry out a human ideal[97] in material form under a rational interpretation,[98] but this occurrence seems accessory to fine art, not fundamental to it.[99] Whatever may be the merit of the fine arts as a stimulus to the value of beauty, they do not, by that aptitude only, enter the Life of Reason.

4. *Art and Its Function*

The Life of Reason implies three broad objectives and art[100] is a prominent factor in approaching them. The first is to provide for continuous improvement in the conditions of human life. The goal symbolizing the improvement is constructed with the assistance of an ideal that reason outlines under the terms of the individual man's situation in nature. This rational ideal guides the current of man's action and is the clue to his progress. The attainment of the ideal establishes grounds that permit the formation of a new ideal and progression to still better things. The second objective is to supply happiness to the human individual. The third is to contribute to the gradual re-formation of the world.

It is understood that art cannot perform these gigantic labors by itself, and, by the terms of the Life of Reason, must integrate with other human pursuits, especially with religion and science. The integration obviously will be rational, and therefore will not be presented in the course of nature but will have to be arranged by man.[101] That art, considered in isolation, may be a good is not to be questioned, and the same is to be said of science and religion. Yet a genuine ethics does not concern itself with any specific excellences of these spheres individually but only with consequences of their rational integration.[102]

In the truly moral integration the place of art is neither trivial nor paramount. To slight art would be to repulse nature and man, to exalt art as supreme and a law unto itself is to be non-philosophical and animal-like.[103] Art has its level that is neither too mean nor too elevated, and belongs in the Life of Reason because it contributes to human weal, imposes sacrifices, and influences other activities.[104]

Yet, intrinsically considered, art has limitations. When it takes the form of fine art, it is not concerned with influencing the world[105] and is not adaptable to a practical objective, for its own beauty is a passion competing with other passions.[106] Only when it is not exclusively fine art may it be a constructive influence as great or greater than science or morals. Although, taken by itself, art is not a stimulant to pragmatic impulses, it may act as a model for practical life. It is especially helpful in showing the way to control sensuous material.[107] And it is by using art as an analogy that science and politics themselves may see how to proceed.[108] In this respect art may be said to embody the rational ideal more fully than either science or morals and to illuminate for the statesman and other citizens the way to the rational goal.[109]

The concrete work of art is a precise symbol of the Life of Reason. And in nature, too, art has parallels. One is seen in the image of the seed. Nature's seed, like each person, has, in the universe of matter, its own ideal and potential life, just as fine art has in the universe of semblance. Though the result in fine art is apparition without existential efficacy, that same result exhibits a formal relation which is a counterpart of the ideal used for an organization having the human individual as its material.[110] The type of internal organization presented by art is the same type the human being will achieve, if he lives in perfect rational activity. In the process of formulating and attaining his ideal he has the formal relations of the work of art as his example. Without this example he remains a brute.

In touching on the significance of art to the state, Santayana observes that art, as a national activity, is invariably neglected because a myriad of social maladjustments claim the ruler's attention. Questions of art are obscured by the urgency of social lesions. Men generally give priority to issues of religion, language, and manners, under the compulsion of a belief that imaginative interests are derivative in relation to material interests.[111] Santayana would redirect this belief to the contrary position that it is the ideal that gives worth to the material.[112]

It may be that art's greatest role is as a force for man's education toward moral ends. Moral life, in Santayana's mode, demands a rational ideal and this ideal demands imagination. Santayana sees reason itself as a kind of imagination capable of surveying man's interests and perceiving how they harmonize or conflict. But, in turn, art is a stimulus and guide for imagination, and the series of psychic steps from imagination to the ideal moral objective is contingent on art for its initial propulsion; in such a context art is a great educator for moral ends[113] and a benefactor of the Life of Reason.[114]

Definitely art stands for aesthetic interests, and if all human experience has an aesthetic side, then art may claim kinship with all human experience.[115] Then, too, the aesthetic value that art produces and the rational matrix that art suggests are of fundamental bearing on man's life, while the scope of art is the entire domain of human assertion. Santayana will not approve the aesthetic factor existing in isolation.[116]

Turning to the realm of sense, man's aesthetic side and the fine art[117] affiliated with it are again of conspicuous import. Sense is readily seen as fundamental to experience and coextensive with it.[118] Whatever is inextricable from sense will bear relation to all experience. Fine art, then, as a concentration and refinement of sense and a stimulation to man's aesthetic faculties, is basically interwoven in all manifestations of human life. As the acme of sensuous organization, fine art serves as a plenipotentiary of sense and a proxy to voice its claims. In the realm of sense at least, its authority surpasses that of science.[119]

Moreover, art does not trespass against either logic or utility, nor hinder their expression and development.[120] The aesthetic power of man from which art draws much of its character, and the aesthetic values which art in turn elicits, give grounds for suggesting that life itself is a fine art.[121] But also, in the best lives, there is a form-giving tendency, an implication of a structure, and service to the rational ideal that point to life as a rational art.[122] Yet, to complete itself, the Life of Reason must go beyond its ideal program. In the end, all of rational art and all of the Life of Reason must have happiness as a consequence or they have been in vain. It is not without obstacles that rational art may be terminated in happiness. Living harmony is required for happiness, and fine art, in the cases where it assumes the role of rational art, is a harmony of appearances, not of existences.[123] Yet fine art, despite its basis in appearances, is unique as a prototype of perfection[124] and is supreme as a guide in realizing form from matter.[125]

Rational art has still another merit that makes it a special channel to happiness; for it is rational art that may remove man from the status and life of a slave. The crucial question for the emancipation is whether or not man's labor follows the rational ideal. If the labor of the individual coincides with the program of a rational life, that individual is free, with happiness as his lot; but if his labor is outside of a rational organization for his case, then his labor conceived as art is merely a source of unhappiness.[126] In a sense, anyone who engages in the Life of Reason may be called an artist, and he is more likely to attain happiness than someone occupied otherwise. Happiness is almost assured by the ability to control and harmonize the diverse tendencies which the Life of Reason presupposes. Such talent is equivalent to reason. Then art, whether construed in its wide sense of all rational action of the organism on the environment or in its narrow sense of the production of some specific art object, has, as its end, individual happiness.[127]

Santayana, in most cases, uses the term art in the wide sense of any making or doing judged meritorious by conformity with a rational ideal. He affirms the interpretation that art is any industry fitting within the Life of Reason and thus allows art a significance that would include science, religion, philosophy, or any other form of human activity. All human operations are potentially art upon meeting the sole condition that they are considered in the light of the individual's interests and in relation to a good which always is allied to a rational ideal. The same doctrine may extend beyond the individual to a larger application in institutions.[128]

Yet ultimately it is more than reason alone which is decisive in the achievement of happiness. Art may lead to happiness because happiness is tightly bound to sense, and sense is much of the raw material of art.[129] Another antecedent to happiness is pleasure and pleasure too usually has a basis in sense.[130] But the conditions of sense are not the only source of happiness from art. There also is happiness from attainment of the freedom that accompanies the creative process. Action, science, and industry, on the level of sense may be rational and agents of happiness. But they are transcended when creativity is present and happiness in freedom ensues.[131] Apparently all men may live according to reason and reap happiness from their programs of interaction with the material conditions of sentience, but only a select group may reach happiness from creativity.

By way of summary, the modification of environment by an organism is fundamental to both the genesis and development of art. Impulse and ideation conspire to give man ideas to apply to his environment with the objective of improving his own life and contributing to progress. Reason acts to indicate a harmonious organization of diverse factors in experience, to represent an ideal moral objective, and to control the activity required to approach this objective. Organism and environment each have plasticity and continuously affect each other, at first spontaneously in the mode of play, and subsequently according to a moral ideal with consideration for utility. The product of the interaction qualifies as art if it has utility, if the producer is aware of the utility, and if the procedure constituting the interaction is transmissible, by either imitation or instruction. Continuous production of art alters human environment and the alteration is a mark of progress. The art to be produced in the future is expected to maintain continuous interaction with the art of the past, and, assuming reason as a guide to the process, the consequence is continuous improvement of the conditions of human existence.

Fine art is distinct from rational art by two criteria: first, since it is predominantly a value of the imagination, fine art lacks the utility of rational art and has no moral commitment; second, fine art makes an abstraction from the real object and rational art does not. Yet fine and rational art are alike in their origin in sensation and reaction to it by the artist, and, conceivably, if the artist is not an aesthete and subscribes to reason, fine art may take its place as rational art, providing it demonstrates some utility. Beyond architecture, however, such a case would be difficult to find. Music and literature originate in the spontaneous exercise of vocal organs; painting and sculpture originate in man's impulse to shape environmental material according to his ideas. In the emergence of a rational art of utility harmonizing with an ideal from a pre-rational art of random play occurring spontaneously, the presence of structure and the faculty of imitation are of conspicuous assistance. Rational art has two stages: one mechanical, wherein a direct encounter with the materials of nature is dominant; the other liberal, wherein there is concern for ideal uses and spiritual functions, following the conquest of nature's materials.

The Life of Reason has three objectives: continuous improvement in conditions of human life, happiness of the individual, and gradual re-formation of the world. Rational art is a force cooperating with other forces to reach these objectives, as well as a precise symbol of the nature of the rational ideal and an educator of men. Rational art simulates a good life in satisfying a form-giving tendency, exhibiting a structure, dedicating itself to a rational ideal, and resulting in happiness and freedom.

CHAPTER V

Embellishments

■

After he completed *The Life of Reason,* Santayana's concern with questions of art and aesthetics diminishes. The occasional writing he attempted in this field lacks the force and constructive timbre of his earlier work. For the most part he clarifies, expands, and re-emphasizes previous convictions without a disposition to try new paths. Perhaps 1912, the year of his departure from the United States, might be a convenient date to record the point where he allows his interest in individual psychology, literary criticism, and rational roads to individual happiness to fade. In a routine way he writes chapters of criticism on Shelley in *Winds of Doctrine* (1913), on Goethe in *Egotism in German Philosophy* (1916), and on Dickens in *Soliloquies in England* (1922), but these are not much more than informal sketches.

After 1912 the chief references to the topics of art and beauty are four in number. These are the articles "Penitent Art" (1922)[1] and "An Aesthetic Soviet" (1927)[2] done in a playful mood but with acumen; a third article, "The Mutability of Aesthetic Categories" (1925),[3] which contains a number of instructive and penetrating observations; and finally, numerous passages within the text of *Dominations and Powers* (1951),[4] Santayana's last comprehensive work.[5] In it he acknowledges that some of his statements in *The Life of Reason* are open to emendation.[6]

In none of these four later sources is there any formidable

contribution to Santayana's existing theory. To be sure they exhibit enough vividness and vigor in handling of material to warrant the opinion that the early zeal for descanting on art and aesthetics was not entirely spent. However there is still not a logical entelechy directing his assertions.

1. *Criticism by Evolution*

In the article "Penitent Art," Santayana offers an appraisal of fine art as he finds it in the twentieth century. His statements constitute a brief, but searching, criticism. He employs the fine art of painting as a vehicle for his analysis, but indicates that his conclusions apply to the other fine arts as well. His remarks approach the status of aesthetic principles and in that light must be held worthy of attention. The theme is deployed in an avant-garde key and affirms the inevitability of constructing new art forms and the impossibility of recovering the character of the art of the past. In the words of the essay: "The notion of *recovering innocence* is a contradiction in terms."[7] A likely implication is that progress consists in being true to one's age. However, the whole piece rests on the assumption that fine art is characterized by a course of evolution wherein it blooms, flowers, and dessicates.

Fundamentally, "Penitent Art" addresses itself to three questions: What is the significance of the term, penitent art? What kinds of penitent art are there? How may penitent art be evaluated?

In treating the first question Santayana invokes the image of the life span of a human female. This female is beautiful in an age of innocence, when she is wholly intent on what she is making, telling, or imagining. Subsequently she is seized with passion and vanity and resorts to all sorts of invention to maintain admiration, and eventually reaches a final stage of reliance on false hair and excess perfume to retain her original charm. There are moments in the last stage, however, when she realizes the folly of her endeavors and pretense and with a tone of repentance disclaims them. She is then a "penitent" approaching conversion to her true status.

The allegory signifies the progress of art. Art, historically, had its age of innocence, when it was beautiful without the awareness of being beautiful; and its subsequent age of self-consciousness or sophistication, when it resorted to "fashion after fashion to keep appreciation alive"; and then its final or contemporary stage of desperation, when some of it remains unrepentant and documentary of a luxurious tradition as well as academic in carrying out ordinary socio-economic commitments.[8] In the art of this last stage numerous contrivances are employed to retain the former elaborate glory, while the occasion of penitence arrives when the trappings dissolve into more genuine forms.[9]

Santayana then treats the second question, which concerns the kinds of penitent art he has observed: that of pure color and that of caricature.[10] In the case of pure color the penance to be performed will be a renunciation of representation that will disregard all practical habits of perception and suppress the understanding.[11]

The objective of any penance is salvation, and the love of pure color signifies that *"salvation lies in emancipating the medium."*[12] This objective excludes as vain "the attempt to depict or beautify external objects." Real material objects of the ordinary kind are ignored in the artist's work, and nature unadorned is accepted as a fit subject for painting. Nature is viewed as "the urgency of life" and as "a hideous strife of forms devouring one another." The painter's composition is often "lights, patterns, dynamic suggestions, sights and memories fused together, hypnotic harmonies such as may visit a vegetative or even mineral sensibility; you become a thousand prisms and mirrors reflecting one another."[13]

In the devotion to pure color the human soul is not lost but is saved. The project renounces attempts "to observe or preserve what are called *things*,"[14] including material forms, moral sentiments, and animal adventures. One result is a purification of the individual sensibility through which nature as beautiful may be beheld.[15] This kind of penitent art permits the painting medium to separate from the conventional image and seek its own glory.

The second kind of penitent art is that of caricature. In this case the artist observes and expresses external things but in a distinctive way. He handles his selected subject matter with a childlike tenderness and with an appeal to a rudimentary sense of life. He relies on "a pregnant hint," or "some large graphic sign," or "some profound caricature." His statement is brief and stops with a fresh, dreamlike rendition that indicates much while reproducing little. Artists of this group believe that things penetrate to the soul not in their material entirety but in some simple large identity.[16] While this kind of penitent art is caricature, it is profound caricature because it sees the invisible roots of men; it sees men in their original animal and puppet-like state.[17] The tender, sublime distortion breaks through the false mask of rationality and becomes a chosen road to salvation.[18]

The third question of the essay relates to the evaluation of the penitent art denoted. Critics are inclined to look upon the penitent caricature as primitive or savage. The association is patently false. The art of the savage is crude simply because of lack of skill, knowledge, and vision, not by intention.[19] In contrast, penitent caricature is a highly refined art. The illusion of childishness it presents even may be overly refined.[20] He who can produce penitent art is no incompetent artist. He may be morbid and ascetic; he may be scornful of self and joyless; but he is not incompetent.[21]

It is in the dimension of evolution that penitent art must be judged. There is a birth and death cycle in the domain of fine art analogous to that in the domain of nature.[22] In the evolutionary prototype consisting of the artists of the late Roman Empire, penance may be identified with the character of the decoration of a Byzantine sanctuary; while in the modern counterpart penance occurs as a study of private sensations, and of the mysteries of sheer light and sound, in the psychological desert which is the consciousness of the isolated individual. Also the trend of detachment from everything except its own medium, signified by the penitent art of pure color, parallels the trend within the contrasting art of music in which singing divorced itself from poetry and instrumental music from vocal.[23]

Painting is merely conforming to an evolutionary pattern when the artist either emancipates his medium or is bounded in caricature by the psychological medium of himself wherein his imagination creates forms in perspective and in character that require interpretation by some fanciful construction and cannot be interpreted as representation of a literally real object.[24] In passing, Santayana includes the subtle assertion that in traditional painting itself "the total composition never was nor ever could be a living image."[25] The traditional painter could offer only what a thing looked like to him in a fleeting instant. The image this painter sees defies captivity, for psychologically it instantly vanishes and the painting is merely its revival by optical tricks.[26] The interesting paradox is that what an orthodox representational painting offers under the category of resemblance is not so much resemblance by literal coincidence as it is resemblance by feeling; the medium of sense does not inform us as truly as the non-cognitive medium of spiritual sympathy.[27] The penitent artist is free from this kind of illusion. He does not profess to purvey an apprehension of literal truth. He is satisfied with his own intuition of "rhythms, echoes, or rays."

2. The Artist as an Aesthete

"An Aesthetic Soviet" is a profoundly suggestive essay. It displays a ferment at work in Santayana's thought about art and aesthetics and attempts to resolve some reflections that, if left to themselves, might seem to be contrary to his usual position.

In "Penitent Art" Santayana chose the image of the course of a feminine life to color his statements; in "An Aesthetic Soviet" he adopts a similar procedure. This time the image is that of a Soviet, "a caucus of comrades," forming a spontaneous union held together by a spiritual bond. This organization is definitely not a political and moral mechanism with force or dogma aiding its operation. Santayana insists that his image must be one of a spiritual spontaneity, free and clear of superimposed institutional machinery.[28] In such an image he wishes to depict all those who love aesthetic reactions and produce fine art. These individuals will comprise the hypothetical Soviet and it will be one unhampered by material dominations and powers; each member will be an absolute spirit, grounded in himself and responsible only to himself.[29]

The aesthetic Soviet, then, collects its members among "fine artists" seen as exponents of aestheticism. They are the ones peculiarly well fitted to reap joy from the experience of the senses and to endorse the vast number of pleasures from the multitude of aesthetically obvious presentations made to the organism.[30] They are satisfied to the full by spontaneous acts and intuitions, innocent and without need of institutional control.[31]

In proposing members for his aesthetic Soviet, Santayana has to exercise discrimination between the artist as a moral and rational builder and the artist as possessing some of the attributes of an aesthete. Speaking strictly, the moral and rational worker is the only individual that Santayana will recognize as an artist. The kind of man indulging in fine art, and acutely aware of aesthetic values, theoretically is excluded from the class of persons denoted artists—although with certain functional qualifications Santayana often refers to him as an artist. However, he is the very man who will participate in the aesthetic Soviet. In this situation Santayana does not give him a specific name, but assigns him all the attributes of what might be called a "fine artist,"[32] to reduce the confusion resulting from the use of the single term, artist, in two senses. Santayana's authentic artist is greatly concerned with craft and practical objectives.[33] His work requires a manual competence[34] and mastery of a communicable technique. Before he undertakes his handiwork, he recognizes that it will have obvious practical consequences and will conform to a preexisting rational dogma. Also this artist labors under patronage, usually of industry. He may experience an irrational impulse and have vestigial flights of fancy, but any resulting images must be integrated forthwith with the material thing that he is fabricating and by that operation be placed under the control of reason. The member of the aesthetic Soviet differs from the rationally committed artist in at least five respects: first, he values an image for itself in its pure immediacy; second, he disavows patronage of industry, religion, or custom; third, he scorns any obligation to follow existing natural models; fourth, he resists conventional opinion of the physical world; and fifth, he omits consideration of practical consequences.[35]

One of the chief uses to which Santayana puts his image of the Soviet is as a setting in which to clarify his views concerning whether or not beauty may be derived from a spiritual as well as an animal base, and if so, how the beauty so derived would be related to his orthodox psycho-physical kind. He broaches the question somewhat obliquely by noting that the Soviet of aestheticism has the advantage of acting in the realm of intuition. The restriction of being centered in intuition prevents harmful conflicts of the animal impulses of the members.[36] Intuition is something totally unsuited to conflict and is quite apart from the power of destruction. As a consequence an aesthetic Soviet never requires any of its members to forfeit something of himself to an external sovereign.[37]

Santayana anticipates the question that if an intuition is a solitary sort of spiritual happening, then there is no denotable generalized adhesive to bind together his hypothetical Soviet, and the whole image is pointless, since what is being proposed is, on its own terms, an anarchy.[38] He overcomes this presumed inconsistency by relating the parable of the behavior of fish. Though living in a pathless ocean and rarely exhibiting companionship, fish nevertheless swim in schools, gather at common feeding grounds, and go by some inscrutable compulsion to the same current. Similarly the gregarious instinct in man asserts itself in his love for beauty; man expects others will join him in celebrating any of his spiritual visions that awaken beauty.[39] On these grounds the image of the Soviet holds.

Santayana has given warrant for unanimity in the exercise of the spontaneous impulses of the members of an aesthetic Soviet and also stipulated that the impulses are specific. He welcomes the question as to how the spontaneous impulses should be able to be both specific and unanimous and for the answer points to the animal nature of man and his interaction with environment.[40] The spontaneous impulse that the artist-aesthete exhibits as something within his spirit is an egotistic illusion. The real source is within the animal foundation of the organism.[41] There is nothing creative about the spirit or the intuitions that play through it; by itself spirit is unable to institute comparisons or correlations among its intuitions.[42]

The animal motivation and direction of spirit, however, is not enough to account for the existence of an aesthetic Soviet, for a Soviet demands an institution to give members a common task and make them comrades. For example, in the case of a Soviet of sailors the institution required would be a ship; in the case of a Soviet of professors the institution required would be a college. Similarly, in the case of a Soviet of fine artists there is an institution required, and that institution is nature itself.[43] An important order of priority in this context is that between an institution and the sentiments associated with it. The sentiments are always the outgrowth of the institution, not the reverse.[44] Soviets, then, cannot be formed merely by free spirits thinking freely and alone, while indulging in creations of transient and fragile fancy. It is fortunate for the fine artist that he is a natural animal and that nature already exists as an institution in which to launch his Soviet.[45]

However, Santayana realizes that his explanation of the structure and function of an aesthetic Soviet has failed to take into account that among the diverse possibilities of aesthetic productions some are attractive to the producer, others are not. The wayward impulse of the artist-aesthete will prefer to construct one effect and reject another, yet both effects are given as aesthetic. The question is what determines the selection. Santayana answers that the basis of an aesthetic preference is non-aesthetic and may be "familiarity, facility, contrast, affinity, chance."[46] Non-aesthetic motivation may be seen on a larger scale in the case of an art style, wherein the non-aesthetic factor is necessity. The circumstances are that an art style responds to some social and material necessity and dissipates when the necessity is removed. For example, the art of making stained glass flourished as a style when boasts of heraldry were in the air and the cathedral was a civic center which included a theology of dramatic representation; the art became defunct when chivalry declined and a puritanical trend in theological observance arose.[47] Without some external non-aesthetic necessity the aesthetic movement from fashion to style is, for Santayana, impossible.[48]

Also, Santayana insists that "creation cannot be creation out of nothing."[49] The effusive fancies dear to the aesthete are apt to disregard the natural movements of the soul and summon an arbitrary image that slights intuition as an animal function.[50] The result will be sterile, for art cannot be cut away either from nature or from a moral world.[51] One concession, and only one, will Santayana make to the kind of artists in an aesthetic Soviet. Apparently, in some telepathic way, their acts and outlook may be instrumental in refreshing the contrasted "traditional artists."[52] Once and only once will he compliment the rejected souls who are not rational artists. In a clause, discordant with the rest of the essay, he writes: ". . . after all the irresponsible aesthetes are the children of light."[53]

3. *Some Contrasts in Interpretation of Terms*

One of the best summaries of Santayana's position in aesthetics is the essay "The Mutability of Aesthetic Categories." Here he presents an epitome of some of the principal doctrines that he has elaborated in earlier writing. Moreover he offers his views in contrast with those of other writers, a step that he rarely takes but that in this instance is appropriate, since he is treating questions in aesthetics ostensibly provoked by the contents of H. R. Marshall's *The Beautiful*.[54] The role of this book within the plan of the article is that of a convenient instrument. For the most part Santayana asserts and clarifies his own views, using a few selected statements of Marshall as a foil. As the term "categories" in the Santayana title suggests, the material covered is foundational to beliefs within the field of aesthetics, and the organization of this material involves a generous use of philosophical discrimination. Santayana's eye ranges over a panorama of aesthetic theory wherein he focuses upon the following topics: ambiguity within the category of the Beautiful within the term aesthetic, and within the category of the Real; varieties in interpretation of the concept, "expression"; and questions of pleasure and beauty, fine art and beauty, production of an art object, and function of fine art.

It is a persistent view of Santayana that categories invoked by the study of aesthetics are condemned to ambiguity. He had written of this belief in the article "What Is Aesthetics?"[55] In "The Mutability of Aesthetic Categories" he reaffirms the belief but uses different theoretical support for it. The first example of ambiguity is detected within the category of the Beautiful as presented by Marshall. In agreement with the Greeks, Marshall divides the Real into the three mutually exclusive but jointly exhaustive categories of the Beautiful, the Valid, and the Good. Of these three categories the main concern is with the Beautiful and the Good. Marshall notes an ambiguity in the Good, since it may be interpreted as including both the Beautiful and the Useful.[56] However, he finds no ambiguity in the Beautiful[57] and endeavors to make the Good exclusive of the Beautiful by restricting the sense of Good to moral good, that is, to good as having to do with principles of conduct.[58] But such an exclusion is not totally successful, for even after Marshall's distinction both the Beautiful and the morally Good will partake of the Useful.[59] Characteristically, Santayana opposes any attempt to make the Beautiful an exclusive category. He points out that for the Greeks the beautiful was always moral and embodied such associations as "the noble, excellent, admirable, or rightly constituted."[60] Moreover, for the Greeks beauty was not an aesthetic category; their aesthetic category was happiness.[61] Santayana adds that in modern times ambiguity in assigning the predicate, beautiful, is seen in the example of Croce, who applies it to designate what is attractive as well as what is expressive.

There is further ambiguity when the term "aesthetic" is considered. The tendency to interpret the aesthetic as being always beautiful or the beautiful as being always aesthetic is nullified by the precedent furnished by the Greeks wherein the aesthetic may be happiness, not beauty, and the beautiful may be moral, not aesthetic.[62] The term "aesthetic" is used in at least three different significations, as illustrated respectively by the examples of Marshall, of Kant, and of Croce. For Marshall aesthetic is sometimes a synonym for the beautiful; for Kant it is a theory of grammar of intuitions without any implication of value, without judgment, and without taste; for Croce it involves a creative intuition, while suggesting an element of attainment or expressiveness without denotation of the beautiful. The Crocean "aesthetic" does not include any criterion of taste or degree of beauty: all creative intuitions are equally aesthetic without being equally beautiful. In the effort to establish univocality of the Beautiful, the factor of the aesthetic merely multiplies difficulties.

Another course toward isolation of the Beautiful may be through the agency of the Real. Over and above the ambiguity involved in the Good and the Beautiful there is the category of the Real, of which they are components. If the identity of the Beautiful is sought and the Beautiful is a component of the Real, then some information about the Real might be helpful in deciding questions about the Beautiful. According to Santayana, Marshall presents the Real as a category of the imagination, as something which within experience has been shown to be so stubborn that it confronts us wherever we turn, much in the manner of the facts with which we are everlastingly surrounded.[63] Santayana seizes upon this conception as an instance of transcendentalism and thereby open to the objections that any transcendental philosophy encounters, one of the chief being that, in its concern with "specious objects and their logical architecture"[64] it ignores its own basis. Transcendentalism exhibits this incongruity: it calls real such objects of thought as are relatively permanent, and calls unreal those objects of thought that are relatively fleeting. This comparison of ways of thought as the test of what is real or what is unreal is not congenial to Santayana. For him the comparison must be between an object in the flux and what is thought about it, not between two kinds of thought. For Santayana the physical object always is more stable than any thought about it. Judged by Santayana's metaphysics, Marshall, in offering a reality under the criterion of a permanent object of thought, ignores nature which is the foundation of what Marshall himself is calling a reality[65] and incidentally fails to advance toward circumscription of the Beautiful.

The predicament of Marshall in treating reality suggests an analogous predicament of the idealists, Croce and Bosanquet, in treating expression. Croce and Bosanquet, Santayana holds, involve themselves in an inconsistency by saying both that spirit is the only reality and that the primary form of spirit is "expression." Santayana sees incompatibility in these two statements, for if spirit is the primary form of mind it could not express anything, since there would be nothing prior to it to express.[66] It is conceivable that the "expression" of Croce and Bosanquet might express nature, but that apparent solution has to be rejected through the circumstance that Croce and Bosanquet do not view nature as primary, but rather as "a non-existent frontier of actual experience."[67] For a modern idealist, Santayana observes, any conditions or antecedents to be assigned to actual experience are "terms thrown out in a game of thought and merely ideal points of reference for logic."[68]

In contrast to the standpoint of the modern psychological idealist another version of expression is found in the Platonic or religious idealist of whom Ruskin is an example. This type of idealist uses the anagogical approach, which assigns divine, or absolute, or objective reality to every form of being and makes everything expressive of the assumed ultimate reality,[69] the point being picturesquely clarified in the phrase that a worm may express the inexpressible.

There also is a romantic version of expression. In this one it flows in reverse order from that of the mystical idealist. Whereas for the mystical idealist expression always follows a direction from the highest reality to an infinity of lower manifestations and is expressive of this highest reality, expression for the romanticist orginates in the effort of any form of life by virtue of a non-cognitive, nether source[70] denoted as Will. This Will is neither natural nor divine, but nevertheless is the reality that is expressed, and the agent expressing Will is himself expressed by the Will.[71] An account of properties of Will is mainly negative: it is not discovered, nor *ab extra*, nor adaptable to formulation; Will expresses the individual natural unit. Santayana is dubious about the romantic view of expression, since it lacks a prototype and also has no existence previous to a given moment.[72] Will disappears almost as soon as it comes to exist, being superseded by an endless sequence of new expressions, each perishing as quickly as the next one displays itself.[73]

On questions of the physiological basis of pleasure and its relation to beauty, Marshall again serves as a convenient starting point from which to proceed to Santayana's own views. Marshall denies that pleasure is a separate psychological datum and postulates it as always attached to "a sensation that yields other qualities as well."[74] He conceives pleasure as a reaction resulting when a stimulus strikes an organ in which surplus energy is stored.[75] Pleasure is discernible as of two kinds: acute and moderate. Acute pleasures are those that are of momentary duration, made so by the discharge of the potential energy producing them; moderate pleasures are those that fade slowly and are numerous and alternate. The constant combination of numerous and alternate pleasures normally occurring within extended durations permits Marshall to assume that there is such a thing as a field of relatively stable pleasure. Marshall then refers to beauty as "relatively stable, or real, pleasure."[76] Santayana disagrees. He interprets Marshall's statement as descriptive of health or of animal happiness and not of a sense of beauty.[77] Santayana points out that the occurrence of beauty requires some image or synthesis of distinct terms and never can be something indifferent in a "field of pleasure."[78] He also corrects Marshall's suggestion that repeated experiences of a thing as beautiful are necessary to warrant designation of the thing as beautiful. For Santayana beauty is something that arises within the experiencing organism in an instant and is exclusive of repeated impressions on the subject.

Marshall's doctrine of relatively stable pleasure is used further to make a transition to the assertion of three of Santayana's long-standing convictions: first, that the study of fine art is distinct from the pursuit of beauty; second, that the production of an art object depends, not on invention, but on technical procedure; and third, that creation of beauty is not the function of fine art.

Marshall had said, in connection with his statement that "beauty is relatively stable, or real, pleasure,"[79] that "we call an object beautiful which seems always to yield pleasure in impression, or contemplative revival."[80] To be beautiful under these terms, as Santayana observed, a thing "must seem beautiful again and again."[81] Santayana believes that while this qualification does not account for the sense of beauty, it may account for the esteem that causes some works of fine art to be called masterpieces. A work of fine art which is a masterpiece may have the fitness to produce pleasure often, says Santayana, but he notes that beauty is by no means an isolated single factor producing the esteem for the work.[82] Contributing to this esteem may be factors such as date, rarity, workmanship, or significance in the history of art. The rank of a Michelangelo or a Tintoretto may arouse a pleasure from interest and wonder without ever involving the condition of beauty.[83] Collectors and connoisseurs do not seek beauty, and a theory of beauty is not a theory of fine art.[84]

Santayana ever is disposed to minimize the association of fine arts with beauty. In "The Mutability of Aesthetic Categories" he portrays the fine arts as an object of study, like any part of nature. The study of the fine arts may have its rewards. It may yield pleasure, it may refine taste, and it may enlarge the student's outlook.[85] But it is not a suitable attraction for a lover of beauty.[86] Santayana here is repeating with variations the theme he stated previously in *Reason in Art:* "An artist may visit a museum, but only a pedant can live there."[87] Beauty does not cohere with study. Beauty arises as something spontaneous, not as something deliberate.

A second chronic conviction of Santayana is that the production of an art object depends on existing technique and not on spontaneous impulse. So once more beauty is excluded where it might be thought essential: it is not a factor in the prescribed operations that end in an art product. "Art is something that can be learned and taught"[88] and broken down into a series of steps that can be measured,[89] and therefore, it would seem, controlled. Some inspiration is allowed to precede the manufacture of art,[90] but the facts are that art begins where inspiration ends.

The third conviction, that the creation of beauty is not the function of fine art, is a denial of the opposite opinion which often is held. If the function of fine art is the creation of beauty, then the beautiful would be divorced from the useful and from nature, and restricted to such predicates as "decorative, monumental, luxurious, imitative, surprising, amusing, wilful or grotesque."[91] Moreover beauty would be something sought. Both these implications are false. Natural objects and useful objects do have parity with the fine arts in inciting beauty, and it is impossible to reach beauty by the act of searching.[92] Yet Santayana does not wish to imply that the fine artists do not love beauty.[93] They undoubtedly cherish beauty and assuredly seek to have it as a response to their works.[94] But that is not the issue. What is asserted is that artists do not, in carrying on the production of fine art, create beauty.

In this essay Santayana once and for all demonstrates the variability of some of the categories used in discourse on the topic of aesthetics, and his analysis supports the conclusion that, within the categories he mentions, ambiguity is rife and that these categories, accordingly, are unfit to mark any definite or "permanent lines of cleavage in the living world."[95]

CHAPTER VI

Modifications

■

For the most part all of the philosophy of Santayana is a relentless development of a few fundamental concepts found especially in his early poetry. It is rare for him to engage in critical alteration of any of his theory, yet in the area of art and aesthetics there are three such cases. They concern respectively the doctrine of beauty as objectified pleasure, the levels of analysis of poetry, and the scope of the Life of Reason.

1. *A Qualification of Objectified Pleasure*

In "The Mutability of Aesthetic Categories" there is an important footnote of some length[1] wherein Santayana qualifies his account of the association of beauty with pleasure as set forth in *The Sense of Beauty*. In this earlier work he states that beauty is a value experience consisting of the objectification or projection of pleasure during which an element of sensation is transformed into a quality of a thing. Three kinds of phenomenal objects, in varying combinations, accompany the process: those occurring through the presence of sensible material; those occurring through the presence of abstract form; and those occurring from qualities associated with the presented material and the form. These three kinds of phenomenal objects represent respectively material, form, and expression as conditions for beauty, although beauty itself, being a value felt, has no components.

Subsequent to writing *The Sense of Beauty*, wherein the features of his theory of beauty were largely psychological, Santayana devoted increasing attention to his doctrine of essences. When, after a period of about thirty years, he referred to beauty in "The Mutability of Aesthetic Categories" the ontological features of his essences are interpolated within the psychological structure of his original theory. The central thought of the emended view is that pleasure is not intrinsically subjective and therefore does not need to be objectified. In taking this position Santayana assumes that "nothing is subjective in experience except experience itself."[2] If feeling is seen as a passing act of intuition, then feeling is subjective. But there is another consideration involved; that is, a term does not become subjective because an intuition of it occurs.[3]

The conclusion that intuition of a term need not imply subjectivity of the term follows from a distinction between terms of thought and particulars of existence. The terms of thought are universals, but the particulars of existence have two states: they are either substance, or passing intuitions of essences. As passing intuitions of essences they represent the encounter of essences by existence, and the consequence of this encounter is a description which remains after the fact intuited has gone the way of all flux. Substance, on the other hand, is the matter and energy met in action by the human organism and believed to exist but not open to intuition.

Most of the universals used in discourse are a result of the organism's contact with the particulars of existence and are signs or names remaining after that contact and standing for inscrutable substances. Pleasure and color are examples of such names. As names they are neither subjective nor objective but are neutral. Being neutral they do not involve objectification. At this point Santayana is viewing pleasure as a universal of discourse standing for some dark substance. Pleasure here is a term distinguished in experience, but the experience is of discourse and its medium of universals. Pleasure is one of these universals. During the moments when the universal is the focus of attention pleasure might be called a subjective object. In this situation, says Santayana, it "does not need to be objectified in order to be fused into an image felt to be beautiful; if felt at all pleasure is already an object of intuition"; and "the beautiful image," he continues, "is never objective in any other sense."[4]

In the footnote being considered Santayana states that his early phrase, "objectified pleasure," was not intended to be taken as a definition of beauty; that beauty is a visionary essence and as such is indefinable; and that objectified pleasure is a phrase which indicates the conditions and manner in which the apparition of beauty arises and vanishes. He adds that the phrase, objectified pleasure, might be improved by saying that beauty is a vital harmony felt and fused into an image under the form of eternity. He also says that beauty fundamentally transports the subject into the realm of essence and that "no pleasure, interest, or admiration becomes a sense of beauty unless it does so."[5] In another work he remarks that "the beautiful is itself an essence, an indefinable quality felt in many things which, however disparate they may be otherwise, receive this name by virtue of a special emotion, half wonder, half love, which is felt in their presence."[6]

This revised view, which places beauty in the context of Santayana's doctrine of essences provokes a number of questions. For example, since essences fundamentally are descriptions revealed when physical existence contacts them, of what is beauty a description? Apparently it is a description of the fusion of the vital harmony felt and the image at hand, rather than of either the harmony in itself or the image in itself. However, from Santayana's traditional position, the vital harmony felt is the dominant feature of the fusion. The process seems to be that, upon entertaining the image of the required object, the organism develops a vital harmony of constituents it possesses as part of its natural history. This vital harmony is accompanied by feeling, which in the context of discourse would be called pleasure, and both harmony and feeling are fused with the image entertained. The transaction is accompanied by a loss of preoccupation with fact and an intuition of the visionary essence, beauty, which stands as an eternal description of what has occurred. The doctrine of essences provides that, when an organism suspends animal faith in the presence of an image, the image is seen under the form of eternity.

In the original statement of his philosophy of beauty, Santayana distinguished between pleasure which could be objectified and pleasure which could not. This point suggests another question: in the later account of beauty is there any need to provide a new distinction within pleasure between one species which may be associated with beauty and another which may not? The difficulty the question presents is that, if pleasure is to be a neutral term like

color, then either physiological or psychological performance would
seem to be ineligible as an index for discrimination. Even so, there
seem to be cases requiring distinction since they involve pleasure in
relation to an essence and are not affiliated with beauty. Consideration of pleasure associated with senses other than sight or hearing
may be excluded, for Santayana presupposes with the Greeks that
only sight and hearing are aesthetic senses. The question then
becomes: within the provinces of sight and of hearing, how can
one separate cases involving pleasure and not involving beauty from
cases involving both pleasure and beauty? A partial resolution of the
distinction is obvious: cases which do not embody a vital harmony
felt and fused into an image under the form of eternity could not be
associated with beauty. But even though excluded from the essence,
beauty, might not some of them be designated with the term,
pleasure? That is, it would seem that there are many essences that,
when contemplated by intuition with the assistance of visual and
auditory organs and processes, are parties to a condition which
might be designated as pleasure, if only because it represents an
illusion of a suspension of the ravages of existence. Discrimination
within pleasure as a name is not as readily achieved as within
pleasure as a subjective state. One alternative is to treat pleasure as
an accessory to the later theory and not an element affecting it
drastically, even though it is worthy of note because of Santayana's
previous concern with it.

A more pertinent question might be: what is the status of the
original material, formal, and expressive conditions of beauty in the
light of the later perspective? The formal condition seems to remain
the same. There is form in any revealed essence and the image with
which the vital harmony and its feeling is fused will exemplify the
formal condition. The material condition is not so obviously re-
tained. Santayana says that "the most material thing, in so far as it is
felt to be beautiful, is instantly raised above external personal
relations, concentrated and deepened in its proper being, in a word,
sublimated into an essence."[7] Here the mysterious existence-essence
relationship occurs: the given material is transformed to essence, but
besides being so transformed it continues in its natural path which is
one of changing existence, whereas the essence revealed in the
transformation has no existence. Santayana's statement is perhaps
elliptical and he may be assuming that it is understood that intuition
of the material will be the agent that will raise it above external
relations by witnessing a description of it which is an essence.

Expression faces a similar predicament. The associations with the formal and the material condition, which constitute the condition of expression, are indigenous to natural process, and they, too, must carry on in their existential character. The presumption is that they are sublimated to essence just as the given material was, although, in the case of expressive data, Santayana is not explicit about such a transformation. The material and the expressive conditions are not intrinsically akin to essence, and their affiliation with it is not seen as plainly as that of form, which itself is close to pure essence.

In the act of composing the vital harmony and experiencing its accompanying feeling, there is a "convergence in the psyche of many assaults and many reactions, from far and near. Some of these influences may come from . . . morality, or . . . literature; some may come from erotic sensibility, from familiarity, from lucidity, from harmony with other esteemed things."[8] Santayana illuminates this point by imagining a visit to the Louvre of a Chinese who does not experience a profound beauty when encountering the Venus de Milo because he is incapable of feeling the "luminous scorn" or "victorious perfection" of the Greek gods. This example serves not only as evidence that deficiency of antecedent ingredients to compose a felt harmony acts to deprive the organism of beauty but also that no physical state of fine art is beautiful or ugly in itself. It becomes so only by integration with a living human organism. Santayana's beauty is something fresh and eternal, never a permanent property of a physical object. The locus of beauty is an indefinitely large number of essences, revealed one at a time to those who can qualify with a felt vital harmony that will contact this external, eternal, but non-existing datum, which however is pure and sufficient in itself before it chances to describe some passing moment in the existence of some organism. Beauty is pluralistic. Moreover, there is no generic primacy within it. The relation of genus and species, or of one and many, does not apply among essences considered intrinsically. There are an endless number of essences awaiting interception by natural process, and among them would be all those which, given the factual conditions, would be descriptive of them as beautiful, and, without the factual conditions, would rest in unmolested purity.

When, in his fertile footnote, Santayana refers to beauty as essence, he includes two significant reservations: he says beauty is visionary and it is indefinable. Accordingly, it is not the commonplace case of essence as constantly encountered by flux. You can indicate the essence which is the yellow of the buttercup or the one which is the blue of the sky. But you cannot do the same with the essence which is called beauty. It has to be visionary, and it has to be felt. Any effort toward intellectual identification of it is extraneous, even though it involves an intuition of form. In Santayana's words: "The sense of beauty is not a feeling separable from some intuition of form; on the other hand, it is a feeling, not a verbal or intellectual judgment."[9] Form is felt to be beautiful, not known to be beautiful. By considering an essence, beauty, as indefinable and visionary, Santayana is taking it out of the class of essences which are encountered solely by means of sensation and intuition. The medium for liberation of beauty seems to be intuition and passion.[10] Then differences in images are not adequate as a basis for distinguishing different occasions of beauty. The condition which is the foundation of variations in beauty is the vital felt harmony. This harmony is a different fact each time it occurs and it controls differences in beauty. For Santayana existence always determines the manifestation of essence.

There is one more interesting difference between Santayana's earlier and later approaches to beauty. In the earlier view, when determining the eligibility of pleasure as an element in beauty, he distinguishes between a physiological center of pleasure and an illusory external one. In the later view, when commenting on the contemplation of beautiful things, he makes a distinction between looking to understand and looking to see.[11] The distinction is reminiscent of Schopenhauer. In looking to understand, one is preoccupied with practical considerations, is in a context of causation with reference to the image of the material object, is thinking in terms of external relations, and is excluded from traffic with beauty. In looking to see, one is lifted out of this utilitarian, practical context, and the material thing confronting the observer is sublimated into an essence. In looking to understand, beauty is absent; in looking to see, beauty has the opportunity to exhibit itself. This sort of criterion for the appearance of beauty has a savor quite different from that of the pleasure references in *The Sense of Beauty*.

2. An Amendment to Critical Standards

In an essay, "On My Friendly Critics,"[12] Santayana revises his former attitude concerning the properties of moral status and universal proportions as requirements for the highest ranking in poetry. The main direction of the essay is a defense against opinions that, in *Interpretations of Poetry and Religion,* his conception of values as independent of existence is fantastic and that there and elsewhere his naturalism is dogmatic. He meets the first stricture by stating that it misrepresents him, since he definitely includes human emotion in all poetry and religion and the values therefrom.[13] Consequently he does not conceive values as outside of existence. In reply to the objection that his naturalism is dogmatic, Santayana says that he is not concerned with avoiding dogmatism in thinking about the universal flux of events which is called nature. Dogmatism, he believes, is unescapable in treating nature, for "every assertion about existence is hazarded, it rests on animal faith, not on logical proof; and every argument to support naturalism, or to rebut it, implies naturalism."[14]

In the course of these replies Santayana compares his earlier and later views of poetry and religion. When younger he looked for a rational justification for them and looked also for their significance in relation to true facts.[15] Of his later perspective he says: "Age has made me less exacting, and I can now find quite sufficient perfection in poetry, like that of the Chinese and Arabians, without much philosophic scope, in mere grace and feeling and music and cloud castles and frolic."[16] Obviously this later position contrasts sharply with his previous preference for moral and rational orientation.

In Santayana's change of outlook toward poetry the question of the character of mind is pertinent. In *Interpretations of Poetry and Religion* he was thinking of the poetic and religious ideas of man and limited their value to what they represented among the elements of human experience. He assumed that "an idea could have depth and richness only if somehow redolent of former experiences of an overt kind."[17] He mentions that he had been taught "to assign no substance to the mind, but to conceive it as a system of successive ideas, the later ones mingling with a survival of the earlier, and forming a cumulative experience."[18] He does not abandon this doctrine of the mind but augments it by an acceptance of a mental substructure, consisting of material and psychical machinery, which he sees with a new confidence as a natural revelation of the existence of a living animal's environment that could be named matter, substance, nature, or soul. The effect of this assumption on standards of criticism is seen by considering that, when natural substance is placed beneath the surface of experience, "the first song of a bird may . . . be infinitely rich and as deep as heaven, if it utters the vital impulses of that moment with enough completeness."[19] The expression of a moral burden of life is not required in these kinds of utterance. Nor for inward force or intrinsic beauty need they rely on conveyance of intelligibility to another person. Poetry may have a perfection in lyrical adequacy and may be independent of wisdom, although not independent of nature. Of themselves poetry and religion may attain a high status without regard for lessons of experience or for a moral program, and may have self-sufficiency without being a specific influence on environment or having any other application.

This newly ranked poetry, even though something imaginative and not necessarily bearing significantly on the outer world, still serves to express natural events, if only within the context of inner growth.[20] Data of the imagination have a point in common with the daily experience of the senses and with the ideas of science in that they may form a human language. In this language all terms would be poetical and all images would be dreams, and yet these may symbolize things and events beyond the language and controlled apart from it.[21] Enlightenment follows as the dream world of poetry approaches natural objects which lend practical meaning to it. At the same time poetry, by its own being, is revealing nature, matter, or the substance underlying experience and is discriminating the rhythms and colors of the mind.

3. The Larger Aspect of Reason

In Santayana's last major work, *Dominations and Powers*, he returns to the topic of art and treats it as integrated with man viewed in the light of his membership in large social and political organizations. In many ways *Dominations and Powers* is a magnification of *Reason in Art*. In the earlier work Santayana was looking at the individual man and all the activities in which this individual engaged in practicing art according to reason, a feat designed to culminate in happiness. In the years intervening between the two statements, Santayana realized that, somehow, in *Reason in Art*, he had not found what he was seeking,[22] that the Greek basis of conduct formulated by Plato and Aristotle failed to take into account many forces that have since arisen in the life of man, especially non-territorial powers such as religion and the relation that future states assumed toward non-political impulses of human nature,[23] examples of which might be the impulse toward art and science. Santayana had not seen the full scope of reason when he had viewed it in the individual life in *Reason in Art*. To the extent that this view was incomplete, it was unsatisfactory. Perhaps, by viewing the influences, that is, the dominations and powers, playing upon human groups, he may see more clearly the operations of reason and discover their nature more truly;[24] if so, he may then be able to describe the path to the "intimate spiritual fruits" of social and political organisms, an undertaking parallel to the one he already had completed in his early account of the path to the happiness and freedom of the atomic organism. Under such an hypothesis, *Dominations and Powers* may be interpreted as the Life of Reason writ large.

Dominations and Powers encompasses all of natural experience, individual and social, within three orders: the generative, the militant, and the rational. It is not hard to see their prototypes in Santayana's early thought as nature, individual impulse, and reason. The generative order is the order of growth, custom, and tradition; it is distinguished "not by its secret mechanism" but by a result, by "the specific trope which nature . . . tends to reproduce, as it reproduces plants from seeds."[25] The human family would be an example of such a growth. The militant order is that of "all voluntary associations that cross the generative order of society."[26] Examples would be political parties, religious sects, and parasitical arts. The rational order is posterior to the generative and militant, not becoming operative until man's immediate needs for self-preservation have been met. The rational order is then the ideal to be made of the free uses of life. In all three orders "mankind exercises its own vital powers either in harmony with the ambient powers of nature or in conflict with them."[27] There is here not so cheerful an outlook as that formulated by the earlier doctrine that "everything ideal has a natural basis and everything natural an ideal development."[28] The new, large "reason" will be the harmony "between the formative impulse of life and the balance of ambient powers."[29] Also "the three orders are interwoven in reality and while the first may exist without the second or third, as in the vegetable kingdom, the other orders cannot exist without the first; and in human history the second and third are also present throughout."[30]

Running through Santayana's three orders are two categories, respectively denoted dominations and powers.[31] Every political and economic system that arises in the course of human history will be colored by the forces in these two categories. Santayana's objective is to exhibit a theoretical instrument whereby some moral philosopher may trace the passage of mankind from one type of civilization to another and "to disentangle the Powers at work in that civilization and mark the Domination that one or another of them may exercise over the rest"[32]—for example, to see the survival of the patriarchal ideals of the Book of Genesis in the militant society of the Book of Kings.

By a Domination Santayana signifies something distinct from a Power.[33] The distinction is not physical. It does not rest on a difference in strength of the force exerted by either a domination or a power but rather on the relation of the domination or power "to the spontaneous life of some being that it affects."[34] To illuminate his point Santayana observes that the same government may be a benign and useful power for one class or one province and may exercise over another class or province a cruel domination. Santayana's distinction between dominations and powers is made from the point of view of a given person or society having its own initial interests but placed within circumstances over which it has no control. Almost automatically these circumstances are divided by the person or society into two classes: things favorable or neutral; and things fatal or frustrating. Those things of the second class, from which there is no escape, are Dominations.[35]

It is against this background of Powers and Dominations in generative, militant, and rational orders that the arts will be considered. To examine the arts themselves within this setting Santayana calls attention to an old distinction between arts that are necessary and arts that are optional. The basis for this distinction was the view that "man lives by bread alone"; accordingly, the arts which contribute food to him are the necessary arts; those arts which do not so contribute are the optional, or parasitical, arts.[36] But Santayana does not wish to press this distinction unduly. Necessary arts also may be found among those contributing to clothing, shelter,[37] and whatever else aids in the maintenance and defense of life, as well as in the use of leisure and the creation of happiness.[38] The arts which satisfy the demands of all these domains are sometimes necessary and sometimes optional, and include a wide variety of trades that require special skill and knowledge.[39] To what extent and in what cases the large group of arts beyond those essential for food shall be allowed to develop is a question to be decided by reason,[40] and falls within the category designated as the rational order.

But the arts themselves, apart from their control by reason, have aspects within both of the other orders: the generative and the militant. The three orders are not separable processes.[41] The arts may be seen conveniently as divided into the species of economic and liberal. Economic arts are such as participate in the economic order of a given society; liberal arts are such as derive their value for what they may contribute to human happiness and at the same time they cannot fail to articulate with the economic order.[42]

In most respects there is no divergence between Santayana's views of art in *The Life of Reason* and those in *Dominations and Powers*. In both, art is seen as originating in a playful interaction of organism and environment; and in both art evolves to a final stage where it is liberal without ceasing to be useful. Santayana retains his fundamental tenet that liberal arts are distinguished by a kind of work done not under pressure as from a master to a slave but "with a vital liberty which studies and remoulds matter in sympathy with its own life, or in ideal variations upon it, expressing human capacity for conception and enjoyment."[43]

Perhaps the main difference between the earlier and later presentations of art is one of emphasis rather than of theoretical position. In *Dominations and Powers* Santayana is quite conscious of the negative and destructive powers of the mechanical and industrial arts,[44] an aspect he slighted in *The Life of Reason*. He also becomes aware of a consequence he neglected totally in the earlier work, namely, that the mechanical and industrial arts conflict with each other, in the sense that the producers of one art product are disposed to crush the producers of another, whether similar to the first or unlike it; that the greater on the less feeds evermore.[45] Santayana traces the basis of hostility among the producers to their motivation by interests and desires.[46] It is the counter-stresses and irrationality of the activities of impulse that precipitate clashes and curses on men. Among the interests found in the organism there are two kinds, one applying to action intrinsic to the organism, for example, singing; and the other applying to action of the organism directed to something outside of itself, for example, cultivating land. The kind of interest that reaches outside of the organism, as in the practice of an art, is likely to arouse proprietary passions, since the artist and his work are dynamic units in the realm of matter and there is inevitably a strong interest to preserve both.[47] In fact this interest may be so strong that it overruns the field of art entirely and extends to viciousness, destruction, and most of the other human woes. The will involved may be one, not only to devour, but to gather, hold, and guard everything devourable. Arts, which Santayana depicted formerly only as objects of respect, now are not invariably a kind of rational industry; they may be pernicious deviates from it.[48]

Santayana's modification of his opinion of the arts seems to correlate with a modification of his standpoint regarding progress. He now speaks of two kinds of progress, one denoted temporal, the other, true. Temporal progress is the advance of everything toward death, true progress relates to a degree of perfection sought within life.[49] Previously, progress for Santayana was something *sui generis*, which, though it might have moral ambiguity, did not divide itself into kinds.[50]

It also is instructive to see that Santayanta is now indicating greed as a prominent motivation of the arts and even tracing greed from its primordial sources in the bowels of nature to its consummate perfection in man. Man may not be able to progress in some ways, but at least he can in the exhibition of his greed. The reduction of man's greed to its simplest components finds him in the image of a worm having only mouth and stomach. But somehow the intake of the mouth has as its consequence the spawning of some instrumentalities and functions that are amenable to stratification on three levels: the first restricted to the body of the organism, a somatic level; the second detached from the organism's body, but externally related to that body as slave to master, or the moved to the mover—it is an environmental level; the third is the mental organization of all the images and relations found in the first two levels—it is a psychic or ideal level.[51] Thus the web of greed may cover most of the conditions under which life takes place. One theoretical curb to the expansion and intensification of the greed exercised in the practice of industrial arts is the existence of liberal arts.[52] The liberal arts presuppose the consequence of human happiness; they use energy for the sake of the individual's life; they carry a mandate of freedom from external pressure; as such they may qualify to diminish domination by greed. But there is little evidence that they are practically effective, for the tide of greed continues to rise.[53] In *Reason in Art* Santayana affirmed a smooth continuous flow between industrial arts and liberal arts. Any indication that one was needed to save mankind from the other is obscure, not explicit. But in *Dominations and Powers* liberal arts alter, rather than extend, the course of industrial arts. However, Santayana is careful to state that the opposition he mentions is among the people who practice the arts, not between the arts themselves;[54] without this qualification the whole foundation of his view of the arts would collapse. He must maintain a position that will permit continuity between industrial and liberal arts, and at the same time recognize opposition between some people who practice industrial arts and the rest of mankind, as well as among the practitioners themselves.

In the wake of this welter of greed in which men would consume each other, Santayana has one more theoretical recourse for security: the art of government. From antecedents in some ways reminiscent of those of Hobbes, Santayana selects monarchy[55] as the kind of government most suited to rationality. In a way, an ideal monarchy is similar to reason conceived on the scale of a state: the monarch signifies the will and the intelligence which composes a harmonious program[56] for the multitude of individual wills and intelligences relying on his art for their own individual rational lives and happiness.[57] Within the monarch's program the awakening of latent liberal arts will be sought, since they foster a spiritual emanation and provide moral sanctions coincident with those of reason.[58] It is characteristic of Santayana to think of a complete art of living as "economic in its actions for the sake of being wholly liberal in its enjoyments."[59]

Music is an excellent example of what Santayana denotes as a liberal art, for though requiring science and art and spontaneously supplying psychic edification, music nevertheless bloweth as it listeth, and whence it comes or whither it goes is among things unknown.[60] The factor of science in music is measure in motion. Nothing could be more thoroughly embedded in physical conditions than music since it has no existence unless some physical instrument vibrates. In the physical dimension music is open to study by science the same as any material event. Yet music also is fair game for reason. In music a rational measure of organization as well as a physical measure of motion is required. To the extent that arrangement by reason is necessary, music is an art. But it is still more. Music is in touch with something cosmic infiltrating through the factor of rhythm and bestowing the privilege of glimpsing the superhuman.[61] All told music is well fitted to be an ostensive definition of spirit and to exhibit the pattern and components any case of spirit must present: organism, raw physical material and science, rational order and art, all these followed by transport to a superhuman atmosphere.[62]

Another old topic brought forward by Santayana in *Dominations and Powers* is the evolutionary stages of the arts. His statements about it duplicate those of *Reason in Art*. The aboriginal stage of art is play or spontaneous habit, wherein unemployed vitality overflows into idle invention. Play may be a rehearsal for life by the psyche, which at the same time modifies both the organism and its environment. From the modification imposed by play on the organism and environment emerges the stage of useful arts, with their economic character; and out of the useful arts arises the final stage, that of the liberal arts[63] with their spiritual character.

Santayana also restates his belief in the continuity pervading the three stages in the growth of the arts. To uphold this continuity requires the assumption of two transitions, one between play and useful arts, and the other between useful and liberal arts. Of the two transitions perhaps the one from the useful to the liberal arts is the more difficult to maintain. Santayana offers three pieces of evidence to account for it: one is the adaptation and sympathy occurring between the workman and his task;[64] another is the association of images that creates a pictorial accompaniment to human actions;[65] and the third is simple human instinct that of itself seems to have either the property or entelechy to serve the human spirit.[66] Santayana readily sees that diversification in living has increased over the ages; but through it all he sees the arts as a perennial weapon of man against matter.[67]

CHAPTER VII

Commentary

■

From Santayana's diverse contributions to philosophy the fore-
going study has selected those bearing on aesthetics, conceived in its
widest sense. These were found to be amenable to division into
three main parts or aspects, one distinguishable as a treatment of
aesthetic experience, a second as concerned with poetry and its
criticism, and a third as a construction of a theory of art. The study
revealed that Santayana, in treating aesthetics, restricts it to aesthetic experience and conceives art as an activity and a product
aimed at satisfying a moral ideal. His theory of art is not explicitly a
theory of aesthetics and his theory of aesthetics is not explicitly a
theory of art.

Although Santayana frequently is considered to be, among other
things, an aesthetician, he himself opposed being placed under such
a classification. He declared that moral philosophy was his chosen
subject[1] and refused to accept aesthetics as a separate discipline.[2]
The conclusion that would follow from his own description of
himself is that he is not an aesthetic theorist. But the evidence
presented above suggests an alternate view. The man who denied
that he was an aesthetic theorist seems to have made a definite and
comprehensive contribution to aesthetics. However, this statement
shrouds an equivocation between a wide and a narrow sense of the
term, aesthetics. In a narrow sense aesthetics signifies psychological
processes and consequences relative solely to the sense of beauty, or

even merely to feeling, and neglecting other psychological functions, such as those involving cognition and rational ordering. In a broad sense, aesthetics signifies a philosophy of art and embraces a diversity of elements, some empirical, others rational, and still others transcendental. It includes theories about art objects, about creativity, and about art appreciation.

When Santayana disclaimed being an aesthetic theorist, he doubtlessly was referring to aesthetics broadly viewed, in which perspective he himself, in the essay "What Is Aesthetics?", saw it as something without definite identity. *The Sense of Beauty* alone is sufficient warrant for the conviction that he contributed significantly to aesthetics in the narrow, or psychologically limited, sense. Even today his presentation of aesthetic experience is followed by some American students and has colored the argument in several books on aesthetics. *The Sense of Beauty* is still widely used as a reference and, in some instances, as an aesthetics text, in spite of being a book first published in the nineteenth century. Both the present essay and that of W. E. Arnett offer grounds for the belief that Santayana's work goes well beyond the psychology of beauty, that he is a definite contributor to aesthetics in any sense, and that he has earned a place in the history of that field. The subordination of his aesthetic theory to moral objectives which he specified is not equivalent to the exclusion of aesthetics from his philosophy.

There was, within Santayana's unacknowledged aesthetic theory, a tacit organization among the elements of aesthetic experience, poetry and its criticism, and rational art. Obviously this tripartition was not taken by Santayana to be a system of aesthetics; rather it is set forth here as an arrangement of concepts held by Santayana in a number of different contexts and apparently unsystematic in intention. For the present purpose the differing elements have been viewed as inviting organization into a comprehensive theoretical structure which would confirm explicitly the proposition that although the doctrines represented may be seen as separate units, they also may be seen as merged into a single body of theory. This body, even if somewhat like a composite, is unified to some degree by mere cogent relationship, by the pervasive telic values of happiness and freedom, and by a natural alliance of feeling, seeing, and doing.

From the time of Santayana's earliest endeavors in poetry, the nucleus of his aesthetic theory was in his mind and from this nucleus each member of what may be conceived as his total theory emerged successively.[3] The doctrines of aesthetic experience were the first to become explicit, but at the same time conceptions of the nature and criticism of poetry and a doctrine of rational art were latent beside them. In the second stage an explicit doctrine of poetry and criticism was proclaimed, and again a doctrine of rational art was incipient in the process. In the third and final stage the doctrine of rational art received full expression. When the gamut of these three stages was run, the scope of Santayana's aesthetic theory was determined. In one light his aesthetics may appear to consist of three distinct segments, but seen in the way of a panorama it appears to have an organic structure.

Generally Santayana prefers to attend solely to the articulation of his innately selected subject matter. It is only in rare instances, such as in "Walt Whitman: a Dialogue" and in "The Mutability of Aesthetic Categories," that he concerns himself with alternate approaches to aesthetic questions. However, he is affected conspicuously by historical sources and is well aware of this fact. He summarized his historical tendency in the words: "I like to lean on the works and opinions of others, as a civilized man prefers cooked food to raw."[4] If his sources are emphasized, his theories suggest a mosaic built from fragments found in the works of other thinkers, a few being James, Paulsen, Ebbinghaus, Simmel, Lipps, Lotze, Fechner, Spencer, Arnold, Mill, Socrates, Plato, Aristotle, Lucretius, Spinoza, Hegel, and Schopenhauer. He does not fail to acknowledge specifically what he received from these men.

Of James, Santayana says, "what I learned from him was perhaps chiefly things which explicitly he never taught, but which I imbibed from the spirit and background of his teaching. Chief of these . . . was a sense for the immediate: for the unadulterated, unexplained, instant fact of experience."[5] Paulsen's influence is acknowledged in the statement: "There was one lesson, however, which I was readier to learn, not only at Harvard from Professor Palmer and afterwards at Berlin from Paulsen, but from the general temper of that age. . . . I refer to the historical spirit of the nineteenth century, and to that splendid panorama of nations and religions, literatures and arts, which it unrolled before the imagination . . . of the Greeks, however, I knew very little. . . . It was with the greater pleasure that I heard Paulsen in Berlin expounding Greek ethics with a sweet reasonableness altogether worthy of the subject: here at last was a vindication of order and beauty in the institutions of men and in their ideas."[6] On technical points in psychology Santayana professed greater agreement with Ebbinghaus than with James.[7] A congenial relativism was found in Simmel's objection to formalism in philosophy, emphasis on instinct and habit as prior to concepts, and disregard for laws and values in history.[8] Lipps's conclusions regarding aesthetic pleasure, value, and objectification have an amazing resemblance to those of Santayana, as these two assertions of Lipps's will attest: (1) "Esthetic pleasure has no object at all. The esthetic enjoyment is not enjoyment of an object, but enjoyment of a self. It is an immediate feeling of a value that is lodged in oneself." (2) "On the other hand . . . in esthetic enjoyment this sense of value is objectified. . . .The specific characteristic of esthetic pleasure has now been defined. It consists in this: that it is the enjoyment of an object, which however, insofar as it is the object of *enjoyment,* is not an object, but myself. Or, it is the enjoyment of the ego which however, so far as it is esthetically enjoyed, is not myself but objective. . . ."[9] It is not established that Santayana drew on the work of Lipps, but it is apparent that the main lines of *The Sense of Beauty* have the same bearing as the position of Lipps.

It is commonly known that the philosophy of Lotze was the topic of Santayana's doctoral dissertation and also that he preferred to work in Schopenhauer but was dissuaded by Josiah Royce. Howgate suggests that ". . . there was in Lotze a distinctly moral outlook which . . . won over Santayana just as he was coming under the sway of Greek ethics."[10] At least Santayana never departed from the viewpoint of Lotze which held that nothing else affirms itself so unconditionally and so immediately in respect to its value as happiness; that only happiness has a valid claim as the ultimate thing to be realized; and that only in regard to happiness does it become absurd to ask why it, instead of unhappiness, must be the final purpose of the world.

References above have pointed to Fechner as supplying the classification of forms used by Santayana in accounting for aesthetic value from form;[11] to Spencer as buttressing Santayana's conviction that the goal of evolution is vital equilibrium between the organism and its environment and that any experience is incidental to animal life and animal passions, which themselves interact with, and are incidental to, the general flux of substance in the world;[12] to Arnold and to Mill as sources for the conception of the ultimate identity of poetry and religion;[13] to the ethics of Socrates, of Plato, and of Aristotle as the inspiration for the doctrine designated as the Life of Reason and its central element of rational art.[14] Then there is Lucretius, whom Santayana called "the great master of my sympathy with nature";[15] of Spinoza he says, "I gathered from him a doctrine which has been axiomatic with me ever since, namely, that good and evil are relative to the natures of animals, irreversible in that relation, but indifferent to the march of cosmic events, since the force of the universe infinitely exceeds the forces of any of its parts";[16] the effect of Hegel is seen in the reference: "I liked Hegel's *Phänomenologie;* it set me planning my *Life of Reason*";[17] and Santayana would intimately accept Schopenhauer in a measure "if we may take 'Will' to be a metaphorical substitute for the automatism of nature."[18] Moreover, Santayana, like every man, had to bear the restrictions of time and place. Accordingly his thought on art and aesthetics is colored by an analytic, functional psychology, a mechanistic view of the universe, and a Darwinian version of evolution.

The non-cognitive character of Santayana's beauty leaves it free from criticism by intellectual standards and not adaptable to reduction to concepts which can be manipulated to voice objections. There is merely a special condition of pleasure, about which it is difficult to be ostensive. The individual subject can decide whether or not he is experiencing beauty, but no one else can do so for him. The theory may be criticized by comparison with other theories or by charging it with omissions, but neither of these approaches touches the theory intrinsically. The theory appeals to one or it doesn't, and there is no way to dissect it mechanically to put it under the wheels of discursive apparatus. Santayana's method of taking a whole and theoretically excluding irrelevant parts to isolate his chosen area for further exposition seems acceptable. He is aware that he is performing an analytic and abstract operation at this point and he specifies that human psychology in its concrete natural functioning has no such division, and that he makes it only to assist communication. He also acknowledges that he "speaks as if the sense of beauty were compounded of ingredients," whereas "sensations are moments of spirit" which cannot endure and cannot be compounded.[19]

Santayana's identification of poetry and religion greatly illuminates the function of imagination in the human outlook. Perhaps the scope and weight that he attributes to imagination is his most distinctive contribution to philosophy. Since imagination is a prime factor in the process of aesthetic value and in the creation of fine art, this contribution indirectly has much relevance in aesthetics. In the domain of criticism of poetry Santayana acted as a critic of himself by deciding to dispense with a universal moral character as a requirement for perfection in poetry.

Santayana also acted as a critic of his own theory of rational art by stating that its original limitation to individuals was inadequate, since social organizations produced their own forces dominating the individual; that art (in his sense of a moral use of craftsmanship) has to be integrated with a background of generative and militant orders within nature and of dominations instituted by governmental edicts; that two kinds of art result, economic and liberal, and that economic arts spawn conflicts motivated by human greed and resulting in a deviation from rationality which the liberal arts may or may not be able to correct. He openly rejected *The Life of Reason* as a book: "The long book in which I expounded what I conceived a life of reason to be . . . was too impulsive, too pretentious, too casual, and based on too little learning . . . and while a rational criterion of moral judgment did underlie the whole discussion, this criterion was not clearly set forth or strictly applied";[20] "the style is, often, verbose and academic, satisfied with stock concepts—'experience,' 'ideals,' etc., and I move too much on the plane of reported opinions or imagined feelings without the actual documents sufficiently in mind."[21]

The influence of Santayana's theory of rational art during the first half of the twentieth century was considerable. The consequences of this theory have been broad and diffuse, extending to a much wider area than the term, art, ordinarily covers. The theory had a politically prophetic aspect that appealed to many people and gave it an acceptance that enabled it to become important in another direction, that is, as an impetus to modern naturalism, whether interpreted in its full philosophic compass or in its restricted sense designated as humanism. Santayana's accomplishment is unique in that he presents a thoroughgoing naturalism, which likewise preserves human values. The theory of rational art, through its provision that individual interaction with a plastic environment acquires a moral character and is instrumental in procuring happiness, may be said to encourage subsequent theories of improvement of human life through realization of beneficent potentialities of environment, approached by control of it. The similarity to the general character of the doctrines of John Dewey is apparent, although Santayana's view in no way is derived from Dewey nor vice versa. The two men exhibit differences in method and in emphasis, but both look to human activity occurring within natural human situations as the means for human amelioration. It is, moreover, true that Santayana's theory of art is more significant as a contribution to moral philosophy than as a theory treating either art in its conventional sense or the nature of beauty.

In general Santayana's aesthetic theory is individualistically relative, hedonistic, contextualistic, and voluntaristically non-cognitive. Four conclusions about it seem to be warranted: (1) he offered a coherent and self-sustaining body of doctrine relevant to aesthetics and art theory; (2) his refusal to acknowledge that he was an aesthetician demands qualification; (3) his aesthetic theory was not developed by progressive criticism, but, for the most part, was spun from one initial insight and one fundamental position by clarification, by elaboration, and by re-emphasis of a nuclear view; (4) most of his theory is not uniquely attributable to him but quite definitely is derivable from his contemporary psychology, from previous philosophy, and from previous literary criticism.

Notes

Subsequent to first references, titles in footnotes will be abbreviated as follows:

DP   Dominations and Powers
GS   G. W. Howgate, George Santayana
IPR   Interpretations of Poetry and Religion
LR I   The Life of Reason, Vol. I
LR II The Life of Reason, Vol. II
LR III The Life of Reason, Vol. III
LR IV The Life of Reason, Vol. IV
MAC   "The Mutability of Aesthetic Categories," Philosophical Review
MS   The Middle Span
OS   Obiter Scripta
PGS   The Philosophy of George Santayana: Schilpp
PP   Persons and Places
RB   Realms of Being
SB   The Sense of Beauty
SELS   Soliloquies in England and Later Soliloquies
TPP   Three Philosophical Poets
WW   "Walt Whitman: a Dialogue," The Harvard Monthly

Unless otherwise indicated all references to Santayana's writings are from the first American edition of the work named.

PREFACE

[1] W. E. Arnett, Santayana and the Sense of Beauty (Bloomington, Ind., 1955), p. 153.
[2] V. ibid., pp. 206–7.
[3] Ibid., p. 204.

CHAPTER I

1 ". . . in philosophy I recognize no separable thing called aesthetics; and what has gone by the name of the philosophy of art . . . seems to me sheer verbiage." *The Philosophy of George Santayana*, ed. P. A. Schilpp (2nd ed.; New York, 1951), p. 20. Now published by The Open Court Publishing Co., LaSalle, Ill.

2 "There is in art nothing but manual knack and professional tradition on the practical side, and on the contemplative side pure intuition of essence, with the inevitable intellectual or luxurious pleasure which pure intuition involves. I can draw no distinction—save for academic programmes—between moral and aesthetic values: beauty, being a good, is a moral good. . . ." *Ibid.*, p. 20.

3 "If happiness is the ultimate sanction of art, art in turn is the best instrument of happiness." G. Santayana, *The Life of Reason*, IV (New York, 1905), 229.

4 "Every artist is a moralist, though he need not preach." G. Santayana, *Soliloquies in England and Later Soliloquies* (New York, 1922), p. 158.

5 "Nothing but the good of life enters into the texture of the beautiful." G. Santayana, *The Sense of Beauty* (New York, 1896), p. 260.

6 "Aesthetic good is . . . no separable value; it is not realizable by itself in a set of objects not otherwise interesting." G. Santayana, *Obiter Scripta: Lectures, Essays and Reviews*, ed. J. Buchler and B. Schwartz (New York, 1936), p. 35.

7 "A reasonable morality terminates in the arts by which human ideals and passion are compounded with experience and adapted to the materials they must work in." G. Santayana, *Egotism in German Philosophy* (New York, 1915), p. 103.

8 "To divorce in schematic fashion one phase of rational activity from the rest is to render each part and the whole again irrational. . . ." *OS*, p. 38.

9 "A society will breed the art which it is capable of . . . but . . . this art will hardly be important or beautiful unless it engages deeply the resources of the soul. The arts may die of triviality, as they were born of enthusiasm." *PGS*, p. 21.

10 *OS*, p. 38.

11 ". . . during a long life, I have expressed in turn different sides of my nature, and developed different parts of my innate philosophy." *PGS*, p. 538.

12 "I was a kind of poet, I was alive to architecture and the other arts, I was at home in several languages: 'aesthetics' might be regarded as my speciality." G. Santayana, *The Middle Span: Persons and Places*, II (New York, 1945), 156. He fails to mention that he also was exceptionally competent as a critic of all fine art.

13 Cf. B. Blanshard, Review of *The Philosophy of George Santayana*, *Philosophical Review*, 51 (March, 1942), 214–15.

14 "I didn't have, and haven't now, a clear notion of what 'aesthetics' may be." *MS*, 156.

15 "Reason was born . . . into a world already wonderfully organized, in which it found its precursor in what is called life, its seat in an animal body of unusual plasticity, and its function in rendering that body's volatile instincts and sensations harmonious with one another and with the outer world on which they depend." G. Santayana, *The Life of Reason*, I (New York, 1905), 40.

16 "Reason is a principle of order appearing in a subject matter which in its subsistence and quantity must be an irrational datum. Reason expresses purpose, purpose expresses impulse, and impulse expresses a natural body with self-equilibrating powers." G. Santayana, *The Life of Reason*, II (New York, 1905), 137–38.

17 "Although happiness, like everything else, can be experienced only in particular moments, it is found in conceiving the total issue and the ultimate fruits of life; and no passing sensation could be enjoyed with a free mind, unless the blessing of reason and of a sustained happiness were felt to hang over it." G. Santayana, *The Genteel Tradition at Bay* (New York, 1931), p. 66.

18 "Natural society begins at home and radiates over the world, as more and more things become tributary to our personal being. . . . There is a primacy of nature over spirit in social life. . . . Things could not be near or far, worse or better, unless a definite life were taken as a standard . . . natural growths [i.e., *natural societies*] may be called achievements only because, when formed, they support a joyful and liberal experience." *LR* II, 137–38.

19 "Reason could not exist or be conceived at all unless a material organism, personal or social lay beneath to give thought an occasion and a point of view, and to give preference a direction." *Ibid.*, p. 137.

20 ". . . the Life of Reason is an ideal to which everything in the world should be subordinated; it establishes lines of moral cleavage everywhere and makes right eternally different from wrong." G. Santayana, *The Life of Reason*, III (New York, 1905), 7.

21 ". . . aesthetic sensitiveness is properly enough called moral, . . . and is more powerful for good in society than laborious virtue. . . . It is *kalokagathia*, the aesthetic demand for the morally good, and perhaps the finest flower of human nature." *SB*, p. 31.

22 ". . . reason in my philosophy is only a harmony among irrational impulses." *MS*, 85.

23 *LR* I, 40.

24 "Reason is not a force contrary to the passions, but a harmony possible among them. . . . except in their world, it could have no point of application. . . ." G. Santayana, *Realms of Being* (New York, 1942), p. 339.

25 "This life of reason is like the crystallizing principle that turns the common atoms of carbon into a diamond; it lends to our animal impulses a nobility which they never had in themselves and which they lose at once if they are liberated." *OS*, p. 272. But neither is reason of any considerable status without the impulses.

26 ". . . pure reason, a reason that is not based on irrational postulates and presuppositions is perfectly impotent." G. Santayana, *Persons and Places*, I (New York, 1944), 241.

27 "Abstraction is difficult for me. Unless I can move with a certain volume of miscellaneous notions in mind, I lose my interest and my direction. I could never play chess: the problems fatigue me without rewarding me." *PGS*, p. 589.

28 *The Sense of Beauty*, 1896; *Reason in Art*, 1905; *Three Philosophical Poets*, 1910.

29 *Interpretations of Poetry and Religion*, 1900; *Dominations and Powers*, 1951.

30 For extensive treatment of this aspect see W. E. Arnett, *Santayana and the Sense of Beauty*.

CHAPTER II

1 "This little work [*The Sense of Beauty*] contains the chief ideas gathered together for a course of lectures on the theory and history of aesthetics given at Harvard College from 1892 to 1895. The only originality I can claim is that which may result from the attempt to put together the scattered commonplaces of criticism into a system, under the inspiration of a naturalistic psychology." *SB*, p. v.

2 An amusing and accurate statement of Santayana's view of the human individual is that made by S. C. Pepper: "a biological organism with a place of his own in the universe and bounded pretty definitely by his own skin." S. C. Pepper, *The Basis of Criticism in the Arts* (Cambridge, Mass., 1949), p. 37.

3 "In such a world there might have come to be the most perfect organization. . . . Yet there would surely have been no thinking, no expectation, and no conscious achievement in the whole process." *SB*, p. 17.

4 ". . . apart from ourselves, and our human bias, we can see in such a mechanical world no element of value whatever. In removing consciousness, we have removed the possibility of worth." *Ibid.*

5 *Ibid.*, p. 18.

6 ". . . values spring from the immediate and inexplicable reaction of vital impulse, and from the irrational part of our nature." *Ibid.*, p. 19.

7 ". . . aesthetic judgments are mainly positive, that is, perceptions of good, moral judgments are mainly fundamentally negative, or perceptions of evil." *Ibid.*, p. 23.

8 ". . . judgments about moral worth . . . are always based, when they are positive, upon the consciousness of benefits probably involved." *Ibid.*

9 "All pleasures are intrinsic and positive values, but all pleasures are not perceptions of beauty." *Ibid.*, p. 35.

10 *Ibid.*, p. 36.

11 *Ibid.*

12 V. *ibid.*, p. 47.

13 V. *ibid.*

14 "But when the process of perception itself is pleasant, as it may easily be, when the intellectual operation, by which the elements of sense are associated and projected, and the concept of the form and substance of the thing produced, is naturally delightful, then we have a pleasure intimately bound up in the thing, inseparable from its character and constitution, the seat of which in us is the same as the seat of the perception. We naturally fail, under these circumstances, to separate the pleasure from the other objectified feelings. It becomes, like them, a quality of the object, which we distinguish from pleasures not so incorporated in the perception of things, by giving it the name beauty." *Ibid.*, pp. 48–49.

15 "Beauty . . . cannot be conceived as an independent existence which affects our senses and which we consequently perceive. It exists in perception, and cannot exist otherwise." *Ibid.*, p. 45.

16 ". . . there is no value apart from some appreciation of it." *Ibid.*, p. 18.

17 ". . . there could be no beauty if there was no conception of independent objects." *Ibid.*, p. 74.

18 ". . . as Spinoza clearly expresses it, we desire nothing because it is good, but it is good only because we desire it." *Ibid.*, p. 18.

19 ". . . for the existence of good in any form it is not merely consciousness but emotional consciousness that is needed. Observation will not do, appreciation is required." *Ibid.*, p. 18.

20 "Beauty . . . is a value; it cannot be conceived as an independent existence which affects our senses and which we consequently perceive. It exists in perception and cannot exist otherwise." *Ibid.*, p. 45.

21 "A first approach to a definition of beauty has therefore been made by the exclusion of all intellectual judgments, all judgments of matter of fact or of relation. To substitute judgments of fact for judgments of value, is a sign of a pedantic and borrowed criticism. If we approach a work of art or nature scientifically, for the sake of its historical connexions or proper classification, we do not approach it aesthetically." *Ibid.*, p. 20.

²² "Had our perceptions no connexion with our pleasures, we should soon close our eyes on this world; if our intelligence were of no service to our passions, we should come to doubt, in the lazy freedom of reverie, whether two and two make four." *Ibid.*, p. 3.

²³ V. *ibid.*, pp. 54–55.

²⁴ ". . . no two men have exactly the same faculties, nor can things have for any two exactly the same values." *Ibid.*, p. 42.

²⁵ "It is unmeaning to say that what is beautiful to one man *ought* to be beautiful to another. If their senses are the same, their associations and dispositions similar, then the same thing will certainly be beautiful to both. If their natures are different, the form which to one will be entrancing will be to another even invisible, because his classifications and discriminations in perception will be different, and he may see a hideous detached fragment or a shapeless aggregate of things, in what to another is a perfect whole—so entirely are the unities of objects unities of function and use. It is absurd to say that what is invisible to a given being *ought* to seem beautiful to him." *Ibid.*, pp. 41–42.

²⁶ "Nothing has less to do with the real merit of a work of imagination than the capacity of all men to appreciate it; the true test is the degree and kind of satisfaction it can give to him who appreciates it most." *Ibid.*, p. 43.

²⁷ *Ibid.*, p. 49.

²⁸ "There is no function of our nature which cannot contribute something to this effect [of beauty], but one function differs very much from another in the amount and directness of its contribution." *Ibid.*, p. 53.

²⁹ "The human body is a machine that holds together by virtue of certain vital functions, on the cessation of which it is dissolved. . . . They do not, perhaps, constitute the whole basis of any one idea or emotion: but they are the conditions of the existence and character of all." *Ibid.*, p. 54.

³⁰ V. *ibid.*, pp. 58–59.

³¹ V. *ibid.*, p. 59.

³² "These secondary objects of interest, which are some of the most conspicuous elements of beauty, are to be called sexual for these two reasons: because the contingencies of the sexual function have helped to establish them in our race, and because they owe their fascination in a great measure to the participation of our sexual life in the reaction which they cause." *Ibid.*, pp. 59–60.

³³ "The color, the grace, the form, which become the stimuli of sexual passion, and the guides of sexual selection, acquire, before they can fulfil that office, a certain intrinsic charm." *Ibid.*, p. 59.

³⁴ V. *ibid.*, p. 62.

³⁵ V. *ibid.*, p. 64.

³⁶ ". . . for a critical philosophy, visible objects are . . . nothing but possibilities of sensation. The real world is merely the shadow of that assurance of eventual experience which accompanies sanity. . . . objectivity can accrue to any mental figment that has enough cohesion, content, and individuality to be describable and recognizable. . . ." *Ibid.*, p. 69.

³⁷ "The senses are indispensable instruments of labor, developed by the necessities of life; but their perfect development produces a harmony between the inward structure and instinct of the organ and the outward opportunities for its use; and this harmony is the source of continual pleasures." *Ibid.*, p. 78.

³⁸ ". . . all images of sense, all instincts and passions are original fictions of the animal psyche, formed according to the structure and conditions of its organs; and it is the free exercise of these organs and active powers that clothes the world with the images and values which we find in it." G. Santayana, *Atoms of Thought*, ed. I. D. Cardiff (New York, 1950), p. vii.

[39] "There is no function of our nature which cannot contribute something to this effect [of beauty], but one function differs very much from another in the amount and directness of its contribution. The pleasures of the eye and ear, of the imagination and memory, are the most easily objectified and merged in ideas; but it would betray inexcusable haste and slight appreciation of the principle involved, if we called them the only materials of beauty." *SB*, p. 53.

[40] *Ibid.*, p. 18.

[41] ". . . just as for practical purposes it is necessary to abstract and discriminate the contribution of one sense from that of another . . . so is it natural that the diffused emotional tone of the body should also be divided, and a certain modicum of pleasure or pain should be attributed to each idea. Our pleasures are thus described as the pleasures of touch, taste, smell, hearing, and sight, and may become elements of beauty at the same time as the ideas to which they are attached become elements of objects." *Ibid.*, pp. 76–77.

[42] V. *ibid.*, p. 69.

[43] "Sound shares with the lower senses the disadvantage of having no intrinsic spatial character; it, therefore, forms no part of the properly abstracted external world, and the pleasures of the ear cannot become, in the literal sense, qualities of *things*. But there is in sounds such an exquisite and continuous gradation in pitch and such a measurable relation in length, that an object almost as complex and describable as the visible one can be built out of them." *Ibid.*, pp. 68–69.

[44] "They [touch, taste, and smell] have been called the unaesthetic, as well as the lower, senses; but the propriety of these epithets . . . is due not to any intrinsic sensuality or baseness of these senses, but to the function which they happen to have in our experience. Smell and taste . . . have the great disadvantage of not being intrinsically spatial: they are therefore not fitted to serve for the representation of nature, which allows herself to be accurately conceived only in spatial terms. They have not reached, moreover, the same organization as sounds, and therefore cannot furnish any play of subjective sensation comparable to music in interest." *Ibid.*, pp. 65–66.

[45] "Artists in life, if that expression may be used for those who have beautified social and domestic existence, have appealed continually to these lower senses. A fragrant garden, and savory meats, incense, and perfumes, soft stuffs, and delicious colors, form our ideal of oriental luxuries, an ideal which appeals too much to human nature ever to lose its charm." *Ibid.*, pp. 66–67.

[46] *Ibid.*, p. 78.

[47] "The beauty of material is . . . the groundwork of all higher beauty, both in the object, whose form and meaning have to be lodged in something sensible, and in the mind, where sensuous ideas, being the first to emerge, are the first that can arouse delight." *Ibid.*, p. 81.

[48] "There is no effect of form which an effect of material could not enhance, and this effect of material, underlying that of form, raises the latter to a higher power and gives the beauty of the object a certain poignancy, thoroughness, and infinity which it otherwise would have lacked." *Ibid.*, p. 78.

[49] ". . . whatever delight the form may bring, the material might have given delight already, and so much would have been gained towards the value of the total result." *Ibid.*, pp. 77–78.

[50] "It is only the beauty of the materials of things which is drawn from the pleasures of sensation. By far the most important effects are not attributable to these materials, but to their arrangement and their ideal relations." *Ibid.*, p. 77.

[51] "The most remarkable and characteristic problem of aesthetics is that of beauty of form." *Ibid.*, p. 82.

⁵² V. *ibid.*, p. 82.

⁵³ "Beauty of form . . . is equally removed from the crudity of formless stimulation and from the emotional looseness of reverie and discursive thought." *Ibid.*, p. 96.

⁵⁴ ". . . however subordinate the beauty may be which a garment, a building, or a poem derives from its sensuous material, yet the presence of this sensuous material is indispensable. Form cannot be form of nothing." *Ibid.*, p. 77.

⁵⁵ *Ibid.*, p. 78.

⁵⁶ *Ibid.*, p. 81.

⁵⁷ V. *ibid.* pp. 86–87.

⁵⁸ "Each point of the retina might send to the brain a detached impression; these might be comparable, but not necessarily in their spatial position." *Ibid.*, p. 87.

⁵⁹ V. *ibid.*, p. 88.

⁶⁰ ". . . if a circle is presented, the eye will fall upon its centre, as to the centre of gravity, as it were, of the balanced attractions of all the points; and there will be, in that position, an indifference and sameness of sensation, in whatever direction some accident moves the eye, that accounts very well for the emotional quality of the circle." *Ibid.*, p. 89.

⁶¹ ". . . the eyes and head do not so readily survey objects from top to bottom as from side to side. . . . The comfort and economy that comes from muscular balance in the eye, is therefore in some cases the source of the value of symmetry." *Ibid.*, pp. 91–92.

⁶² ". . . symmetry appeals to us through the charm of recognition and rhythm. When the eye runs over a facade, and finds the objects that attract it at equal intervals, an expectation, like the anticipation of an inevitable note or required word, arises in the mind." *Ibid.*, p. 92.

⁶³ ". . . unity cannot be absolute and be a form; a form is an aggregation, it must have elements, and the manner in which the elements are combined constitutes the character of the form. A perfectly simple perception, in which there was no consciousness of the distinction and relation of parts, would not be a perception of form; it would be a sensation." *Ibid.*, p. 96.

⁶⁴ V. *ibid.*, p. 97.

⁶⁵ *Ibid.*, p. 96.

⁶⁶ "Form . . . does not appeal to the unattentive; they get from objects only a vague sensation which may in them awaken extrinsic associations; they do not stop to survey the parts or to appreciate their relation, and consequently are insensible to the various charms of various unifications; they can find in objects only the value of material or of function, not that of form." *Ibid.*

⁶⁷ In one of his rare footnotes Santayana states that his classification of forms is derived from Fechner. The footnote reads: "Cf. Fechner, *Vorschule der Aesthetik*, Erster Teil, S73, a passage by which the following classification of forms was first suggested." *Ibid.*, p. 97.

⁶⁸ V. *ibid.*

⁶⁹ "A distinction and association, or an inference, is a direct experience, a sensible fact; but it is the experience of a process, of a motion between two terms, and a consciousness of their coexistence and distinction; it is a feeling of relation. Now the sense of space is a feeling of this kind; the essence of it is the realization of a variety of directions and possible motions, by which the relation of point to point is vaguely but inevitably given." *Ibid.*, p. 98.

⁷⁰ *Ibid.*

⁷¹ "The perception of extension is . . . of the most rudimentary kind. It is merely *Auseinandersein* and we might call it the *materia prima* of form, were it

not capable of existing without further determination. For we can have the sense of space without the sense of boundaries. . . ." *Ibid.*

72 V. *ibid.,* p. 99.

73 V. *ibid.,* pp. 98–99.

74 ". . . this effect of surface is not necessarily an effect of material or color. . . ." *Ibid.,* p. 99.

75 V. *ibid.,* p. 100.

76 *Ibid.,* p. 103.

77 V. *ibid.*

78 V. *ibid.*

79 V. *ibid.,* p. 104.

80 "The more indeterminate the object, the greater share must subjective forces have in determining our perception; for . . . every perception is in itself perfectly specific, and can be called indefinite only in reference to an abstract ideal which it is expected to approach." *Ibid.,* p. 113.

81 "Every cloud has just the outline it has, although we may call it vague, because we cannot classify its form under any geometrical or animal species; it would be first definitely a whale, and then would become indefinite until we saw our way to calling it a camel." *Ibid.*

82 "Our apperception of form varies not only with our constitution, age, and health, as does the appreciation of sensuous values, but also with our education and genius." *Ibid.*

83 V. *ibid.,* p. 131.

84 "The indeterminate in form is also indeterminate in value. It needs completion by the mind of the observer and as this completion differs, the value of the result must vary. An indeterminate object is therefore beautiful to him who can make it so, and ugly to him who cannot. . . . The indeterminate object therefore requires an active and well-equipped mind. . . ." *Ibid.,* p. 145.

85 V. *ibid.,* p. 136.

86 V. *ibid.,* p. 145.

87 V. *ibid.,* p. 114.

88 V. *ibid.,* pp. 114–15.

89 V. *ibid.,* p. 115.

90 ". . . this is the first thing in the value of a form, the value of the type as such; the second and more important element is the relation of the particular impression to the form under which it is apperceived. This determines the value of the object as an example of its class." *Ibid.*

91 V. *ibid.,* pp. 117, 118, 120.

92 V. *ibid.,* p. 122.

93 V. *ibid.,* pp. 128–29.

94 V. *ibid.,* p. 145.

95 V. *ibid.,* p. 169.

96 "The main effect of language consists in its meaning, in the ideas which it expresses. But no expression is possible without a presentation, and this presentation must have a form. This form of the instrument of expression is itself an element of effect. . . ." *Ibid.,* p. 167.

97 "Certain systems of atoms move together as units; and these organisms reproduce themselves and recur so often in our environment, that our senses become accustomed to view their parts together. Their form becomes a natural and recognizable one." *Ibid.,* p. 152.

98 V. *ibid.,* pp. 152–53.

99 V. *ibid.,* p. 154.

100 "Utility . . . organizes the material world into definite species and individuals." *Ibid.,* p. 155.

[101] V. *ibid.*, pp. 156–57.

[102] ". . . although every useful form is capable of proportion and beauty . . . we cannot say that this beauty is always potentially equal. . . . an iron bridge . . . will probably never . . . equal a bridge of stone." *Ibid.*, p. 163.

[103] V. *ibid.*, p. 162.

[104] V. *ibid.*, p. 164.

[105] "We have . . . studied the sense of beauty in what seem to be its fundamental classifications. . . . In surveying so broad a field we stand in need of some classification and subdivision. . . . But aesthetic feeling itself has no parts." *Ibid.*, pp. 266–67.

[106] V. *ibid.*, p. 193.

[107] "The pleasure of association is an immediate feeling which we account for by its relation to a feeling in the past, or to cerebral structure modified by a former experience; just as memory itself, which we explain by a reference to the past is a peculiar complication of present consciousness." *Ibid.*, p. 201.

[108] *Ibid.*, p. 193.

[109] "Expression then differs from material or formal value only . . . in its origin. Physiologically, they are both pleasurable radiations of a given stimulus; mentally, they are both values incorporated in an object." *Ibid.*, p. 195.

[110] *Ibid.*

[111] ". . . if expression were constituted by the external relation of object with object, everything would be expressive equally, indeterminately, and universally. The flower in the crannied wall would express the same thing as the bust of Caesar or the *Critique of Pure Reason.*" *Ibid.*, p. 196.

[112] "What constitutes the individual expressiveness of . . . things is the circle of thoughts allied to each in a given mind; my words, for instance, express the thoughts which they actually arouse in the reader; they may express more to one man than to another, and to me they may have expressed more or less than to you." *Ibid.*, p. 196.

[113] V. *ibid.*, p. 197.

[114] ". . . the expression of utility . . . is found whenever the second term is the idea of something of practical advantage to us, the premonition of which brings satisfaction; and this satisfaction prompts an approval of the presented object." *Ibid.*, p. 208.

[115] "There is no reason why cost, or the circumstances which are its basis, should not . . . heighten the tone of consciousness, and add to the pleasure with which we view an object." *Ibid.*, p. 212.

[116] "Art does not seek out the pathetic, the tragic, and the absurd; it is life that has . . . enlisted art in their service, to make the contemplation of them . . . at least as tolerable as possible." *Ibid.*, p. 221.

[117] V. *ibid.*, p. 222.

CHAPTER III

[1] Comparing his early poetry and later philosophy, Santayana remarks: "I think the discerning reader will probably prefer the later prose versions of my philosophy. I prefer them myself, as being more broadly based, saner, more humorous. Yet if he is curious in the matter he may find the same thing here nearer to its fountain-head, in its accidental early setting, and with its most authentic personal note.

"For, as to the subject of these poems, it is simply my philosophy in the making." *Poems: Selected by the Author and Revised* (New York, 1928), p. xii.

[2] There is still another manifestation of the aesthetic dimension of Santayana's thought. It is in his doctrine of essences, which is outside of the objec-

tives of this study. The doctrine, regardless of an element of aesthetic motivation, is dominantly ontological and epistemological. Its aesthetic side has been explicated well in W. E. Arnett, *Santayana and the Sense of Beauty.*

[3] In *Literature and Dogma* Arnold had presented religion as "morality touched by emotion," and in *Culture and Anarchy* he viewed the best Greek art, religion, and poetry as one and the same. John Stuart Mill had stated the position Santayana adopted even more exactly than Arnold: "Religion and poetry address themselves . . . to the same part of the human constitution: they both supply the same want, that of ideal conceptions grander and more beautiful than we see realized in the prose of human life." *Three Essays on Religion* (New York, 1884), p. 103, quoted by G. W. Howgate, *George Santayana* (Philadelphia, 1938).

[4] "There was one lesson, however, which I was readier to learn, not only at Harvard from Professor Palmer and afterwards at Berlin from Paulsen, but from the general temper of that age well represented for me . . . by the works of Taine and of Matthew Arnold—I refer to the historical spirit of the nineteenth century, and to that splendid panorama of nations and religions, literatures and arts, which it unrolled before the imagination." *PGS*, p. 9.

[5] ". . . understanding, as we have defined it, is itself a kind of imagination. . . ." G. Santayana, *Interpretations of Poetry and Religion* (New York, 1900), p. 7.

[6] "Of the five senses three are of little use in the formation of permanent notions. . . ." *Ibid.*, pp. 1–2.

[7] Cf. *ibid.*, p. 2.

[8] *Ibid.*

[9] *Ibid.*, p. 5.

[10] "The sphere of common sense and science is concentric with the sphere of fancy; both move in virtue of the same imaginative impulses." *Ibid.*

[11] "The eventual distinction between intelligence and imagination is ideal; it arises where we discriminate various functions in a life that is dynamically one." *Ibid.*

[12] *Ibid.*

[13] ". . . profounder minds yield to the imagination because . . . these minds . . . are capable of feeling the greatness of the problems of life and the inadequacy of the understanding to solve them." *Ibid.*, p. 6.

[14] ". . . the impassioned soul must pass beyond the understanding or go unsatisfied." *Ibid.*

[15] V. *ibid.*

[16] *Ibid.*, p. 7.

[17] ". . . the imagination has not misled us. . . . on the contrary . . . in the given instances [i.e., prophecy, revelation, and philosophic reason] the imagination has hit upon an ultimate truth." *Ibid.*

[18] ". . . understanding, as we have defined it, is itself a kind of imagination, an imagination prophetic of experience, a spontaneity of thought by which the science of perception is turned into the art of life." *Ibid.*, pp. 7–8.

[19] ". . . imagination is an irresponsible principle; its rightness is an inward rightness, and everything in the real world may turn out to be disposed otherwise than as it would wish. . . ." *Ibid.*, p. 10.

[20] *Ibid.*, pp. 7–8.

[21] "The imagination, even when its premonitions are not wholly justified by subsequent experience, has . . . a noble role to play in the life of man. Without it his thoughts would be not only far too narrow to represent, although it were symbolically, the greatness of the universe, but far too narrow even to

render the scope of his own life and the conditions of his practical welfare."
Ibid., p. 8.

[22] "To indulge the imagination is to express the universal self, the common
and contagious element in all individuals. . . . to repress it is to chill the soul,
so that even the clearest perception of the truth remains without the joy and
impetuosity of conviction.
"The part played by the imagination is . . . indispensable." *Ibid.*, pp. 9–10.

[23] "Wielding a great power . . . the imagination may abuse a great force.
. . . Our imaginative preconceptions are then obstacles to the perception of
fact and of rational duty; the faith that stimulated our efforts . . . multiplies
our wanderings. The too hasty organization of our thoughts becomes the cause
of their more prolonged disorganization. . . . And as we love our hopes, and
detest the experience that seems to contradict them, we add fanaticism to our
confusion. . . . The habits of the imagination, in conflict with the facts of
sense, thus come to cloud science with passion, with fiction, with sentimental
prejudice." *Ibid.*, pp. 10–11.

[24] *Ibid.*, p. 12.

[25] *V. ibid.*

[26] *V. ibid.*, pp. v–vi.

[27] "This idea is that religion and poetry are identical in essence, and differ
merely in the way in which they are attached to practical affairs. Poetry is
called religion when it intervenes in life, and religion, when it merely supervenes upon life, is seen to be nothing but poetry." *Ibid.*, p. v.

[28] "Religion is poetry become the guide of life, poetry substituted for science
or supervening upon it as an approach to the highest reality. Poetry is religion
allowed to drift, left without points of application in conduct and without an
expression in worship and dogma. . . ." *Ibid.*, p. 289.

[29] "Poetry raised to its highest power is then identical with religion grasped
in its inmost truth; at their point of union both reach their utmost purity and
beneficence, for then poetry loses its frivolity and ceases to demoralize, while
religion surrenders its illusions and ceases to deceive." *Ibid.*, p. 290.

[30] *V. ibid.*, pp. 287–88.

[31] *V. ibid.*, p. 288.

[32] *V. ibid.*

[33] *V. ibid.*, p. 261.

[34] "Our logical thoughts dominate experience only as the parallels and
meridians make a checker-board of the sea. They guide our voyage without
controlling the waves, which toss for ever in spite of our ability to ride over
them to our chosen ends. Sanity is a madness put to good uses; waking life is a
dream controlled." *Ibid.*

[35] "The link that binds together the ideas, . . . which his [the poet's] wit
assimilates, is most often the link of emotion." *Ibid.*, p. 263.

[36] ". . . the first element which the intellect rejects in forming its ideas of
things is the emotion which accompanies the perception; and the emotion is the
first thing the poet restores." *Ibid.*, p. 262.

[37] *V. ibid.*, p. 263.

[38] "The poet's art is to a great extent the art of intensifying emotions by
assembling the scattered objects that naturally arouse them. He sees the affinities of things by seeing their common affinities with passion." *Ibid.*, p. 263.

[39] *V. ibid.*, p. 263.

[40] *V. ibid.*, p. 261.

[41] "Our descent into the elements of our being is then justified by our
subsequent freer ascent toward its goal; we revert to sense only to find food for
reason; we destroy conventions only to construct ideals." *Ibid.*, p. 270.

42 "The great function of poetry . . . is precisely this: to repair to the material of experience, seizing hold of the reality of sensation and fancy beneath the surface of conventional ideas, and then out of that living but indefinite material to build new structures, richer, finer, fitter to the primary tendencies of our nature, truer to the ultimate possibilities of the soul." *Ibid.*

43 "Science and common sense are themselves in their way poets of no mean order, since they take the material of experience and make out of it a clear, symmetrical, and beautiful world; the very propriety of this art, however, has made it common." *Ibid.*

44 It is instructive to observe that Santayana is willing to allow pure science and mathematics figuratively to be objects of poetic criticism. He places them in the next to highest rank within his own critical hierarchy, above sensuous versification and also above romantic expression: ". . . even as it is, a scientific and mathematical vision has a higher beauty than the irrational poetry of sensation and impulse, which merely tickles the brain, like liquor, and plays upon our random imaginative lusts." *Ibid.* This passage is consistent with Santayana's rational ideal and his conviction that "the function of poetry, like that of science, can only be fulfilled by the conception of harmonies that become clearer as they grow richer." *Ibid.*, p. 283.

45 V. *ibid.*, p. 271.

46 *Ibid.*

47 ". . . the images rejected by practical thought, and the emotions ignored by it, are so marshalled as to fill the mind with a truer and intenser consciousness of its memorable experience." *Ibid.*, pp. 271–72.

48 ". . . one principle is present throughout [poetry]—the principle of Beauty—the art of assimilating phenomena, whether words, images, emotions, or systems of ideas, to the deeper innate cravings of the mind." *Ibid.*, p. 272.

49 V. *ibid.*, p. 276.

50 ". . . the passions are naturally blind, and the poverty of the imagination, when left alone, is absolute." *Ibid.*, p. 277.

51 "It was a capital error in Fichte and Schopenhauer to assign essential fertility to the will in the creation of ideas. They mistook, as human nature will do . . . an ideal for a reality: and because they saw how much the will clings to its objects, how it selects and magnifies them, they imagined that it could breed them out of itself." *Ibid.*, pp. 277–78.

52 V. *ibid.*, p. 277.

53 ". . . the single emotion, the fortuitous dream, launched by the poet into the world of recognizable and immortal forms, looks in that world for its ideal supports and affinities. It must find them or else be blown back among the ghosts." *Ibid.*, p. 284.

54 *The Harvard Monthly,* X (May, 1890), 85–92.

55 *The Philosophical Review,* XIII (May, 1904), 320–27.

56 "He [the poet] tells you how in another country, perhaps, he felt what you are feeling now, as he watched the spring of another year. That is the best part of the pleasure, to know it's human and that all men have had it in common from Adam down." *WW,* p. 85.

57 " [Whitman cannot write English] according to the English department [of Harvard University]. But that is a local standard. Could Homer pass an examination in Goodwin's moods and tenses?" *Ibid.*, p. 86.

58 ". . . when English becomes a dead language and nothing survives but *Leaves of Grass,* Whitman's style will be above criticism. But now English has the misfortune of being in use. A man can't make it to suit his fancy, and if he

won't trouble himself to write the language of his fellows, he can't expect them to learn his." *Ibid.*

59 ". . . he [Whitman] produces a new effect, he gives you a new sensation. . . . to learn a method of expression is to become insensible to all it can't express. The schools don't teach us to paint what we see, but to see what others have painted." *Ibid.*

60 "When people are fascinated by the extravagant, they show they haven't experience and training enough to appreciate what is sane and solid. Would you make no distinction between the normal and the human and the eccentric and the perverse? . . . your geniuses, you think, musn't submit to standards . . . but if originality is genius there are more great men at Somerville than at Cambridge. You can't get over the difference between sense and nonsense. . . . Any one can produce a new effect when fools are impressed by his blunders." *Ibid.*, pp. 86–87.

61 ". . . he [Whitman] mentions all sorts of things and says nothing about them." *Ibid.*, p. 87.

62 "You may laugh at his catalogues of objects, at his enumeration of places. But the hurrying of these images through the mind gives me a sense of space, of a multiplicity of things spread endlessly around me. I become aware of the life of millions of men, of great stretches of marsh, desert, and ocean." *Ibid.*

63 "Science is interesting and if you can manage to make poetry out of it we shall have the first poetry in the world not resting on illusion." *Ibid.*, p. 88.

64 ". . . the illusion is what is poetic, and the fact is so only when in fancy we assimilate it to the fiction. . . . The reason why Walt Whitman is ridiculous is that he talks of real objects as if they could enter into poetry at all. It isn't art to point to objects, nor poetry to turn out 'chants of Ohio, Indiana, Illinois, Wisconsin, Iowa, and Minnesota.' Poetry deals with sensuous attractions found nowhere on the map. To see them you must have a passport into fairyland." *Ibid.*

65 "The trouble with the German sort of criticism is that it isn't satisfied with the fact, but goes in search of a theory, as if a theory could be anything real and ultimate, or more than the flight of the soul from perception to perception, from emotion to emotion, on which alone she can alight to find rest and truth." *Ibid.*

66 ". . . beauty is everywhere, if we only had the genius to see it. . . . If some objects seem to you poetic rather than others, if Venice can be apostrophized and Oshkosh is unmentionable, it's because habit makes it easier to idealize them. This beauty has been pointed out so often that we know it by heart. But what merit is it to repeat the old tricks and hum the old tunes?" *Ibid.*, p. 89.

67 "Whitman would teach you, if you would only read him, to see in things their intrinsic nature and life, rather than the utility they may have for one another. That is his great merit, his sublime justice. It is a kind of profound piety that recognizes the life of everything in nature, and spares it, and worships its intrinsic worth. There is something brutal and fatuous in the habit we commonly have of passing the parts of nature in review and pronouncing them good or bad according to the effect they have on our lives." *Ibid.*, p. 90.

68 "It isn't immoral to call a spade a spade, but it is immoral to treat life as a masquerade, as a magic pantomime in which acts have no consequences and happiness and misery don't exist." *Ibid.*, p. 91.

69 ". . . good and evil, although not equally pleasant to experience, are equally interesting to look at. Is it wrong to enjoy our misery when its distance from us makes contemplation of it possible? How else can the gods have been happy?" *Ibid.*

70 "The world is so heavenly to him [the enraptured poet] that he finds nothing to do in it." *Ibid.*

71 "What better thing is there for a man than to remember now and then that the stars are laughing at him, to renounce his allegiance to his own preferences and passions and by understanding to enter into those of other men?" *Ibid.*

72 *OS*, p. 32.

73 *Ibid.*

74 V. *ibid.*, pp. 32–33.

75 V. *ibid.*, p. 33.

76 V. *ibid.*, pp. 33–34.

77 *Ibid.*, p. 34.

78 *Ibid.*

79 V. *ibid.*, p. 35.

80 V. *ibid.*

81 V. *ibid.*, p. 36.

82 V. *ibid.*, pp. 35–36.

83 "Reason suffers us to approve with no part of our nature what is offensive to any other part. . . ." *Ibid.*, p. 36. In "What Is Aesthetics?" Santayana prestates the central concepts and assumptions of *The Life of Reason*.

84 *Ibid.*, p. 36.

85 *Ibid.*, p. 37.

86 V. *ibid.*

87 V. *ibid.*

88 V. *ibid.*, p. 38.

89 *Ibid.* In contrast to Santayana's position, Hugo Münsterberg, his closest friend among the Harvard faculty members, held that the only way a psychic state could be genuinely aesthetic was in isolation from all others.

90 V. *ibid.*

91 ". . . side by side with pure aestheticism . . . we should have to admit the undeniable beauties of the non-aesthetic, of everything that was fit, lucid, beneficent, or profound." *Ibid.*, p. 39.

92 V. *ibid.*

93 *Ibid.*

94 V. *ibid.*

95 *Ibid.*

96 G. Santayana, *Three Philosophical Poets* (Cambridge, Mass., 1910), p. 8.

97 *IPR*, p. 7.

98 *TPP*, p. 8.

99 "The reasonings and investigations of philosophy are arduous. . . . But the vision of philosophy is sublime. The order it reveals in the world is something beautiful, tragic, sympathetic to the mind, and just what every poet, on a small or on a large scale, is always trying to catch." *Ibid.*, p. 10. The allusion to the Greek concepts of *dianoia* and *theoria* is obvious.

100 V. *ibid.*, pp. 10–11.

101 "They [reasoning and investigation] terminate in insight, or what in the noblest sense of the word may be called *theory, theoria*—a steady contemplation of all things in their order and worth. Such contemplation is imaginative. . . . A philosopher who attains it is, for the moment, a poet, and a poet who turns his practised and passionate imagination on the order of all things, or on anything in the light of the whole, is for that moment a philosopher." *Ibid.*, p. 11.

102 *Ibid.*, p. 12.

103 V. *ibid.*

104 *Ibid.*

105 *Ibid.*, p. 13.

106 *Ibid.*

107 "When we feel the poetic thrill, is it not that we find sweep in the concise and depth in the clear, as we might find all the lights of the sea in the water of a jewel? And what is a philosophic thought but such an epitome?" *Ibid.*

108 *Ibid.*

109 V. *ibid.*

110 *Ibid.*

111 "Poetry . . . is not poetical for being short-winded or incidental, but, on the contrary, for being comprehensive and having range." *Ibid.*, p. 14.

112 "As in a supreme dramatic crisis all our life seems to be focused in the present, and used in colouring our consciousness and shaping our decisions, so for each philosophic poet the whole world of man is gathered together; and he is never so much a poet as when, in a single cry, he summons all that has affinity to him in the universe, and salutes his ultimate destiny. . . . The height of poetry is to speak the language of the gods." *Ibid.*

113 *Ibid.*

114 V. *ibid.*, p. 21.

115 "To perceive universal mutation, to feel the vanity of life, has always been the beginning of seriousness. . . . Prior to that everything is barbarous, both in morals and in poetry; for until then mankind has not learned to renounce anything, has not outgrown the instinctive egotism and optimism of the young animal, and has not removed the centre of its being or of its faith, from the will to the imagination." *Ibid.*, pp. 23–24. It is a fundamental in Santayana's doctrines of both aesthetic criticism and aesthetic production that the will cannot create anything.

116 "Any comprehensive picture of nature and destiny . . . must arouse emotion, and in a reflective and vivid mind must inspire poetry—for what is poetry but emotion, fixing and colouring the objects from which it springs?" *Ibid.*, p. 62.

117 V. *ibid.*, p. 68.

118 This kind of nexus between emotion and the universe is quite consistent with the metaphysics of Lotze, which found laws of mechanism and the operation of the intellect inadequate for apprehending reality because neither could account for coherence among things, which however could be apprehended by feeling. "If we would hold reality in our grasp then it is not to thought we must go but to the activities of feeling and will. . . . these same activities must be the root of the world order, and will give us the clue to the nature of that order." E. E. Thomas, *Lotze's Theory of Reality* (London, 1921), p. 174.

119 "If there are no atoms, at least there must be habits of nature, or laws of evolution, or dialectics of progress, or decrees of providence, or intrusions of chance; and before these equally external and groundless powers we must bow, as Lucretius bowed to his atoms." *TPP*, p. 69.

120 V. *ibid.*, p. 70.

121 "A mind persuaded that it lives among things that, like words, are essentially significant and that what they signify is the magic attraction, called love, which draws all things after it, is a mind poetic in its intuition, even if its language be prose." *Ibid.*, pp. 102–3.

122 "[Dante] accomplishes the feat which he attributes to the Creator; he evokes a material world to be the fit theatre for moral attitudes." *Ibid.*, p. 120.

123 "To object to theory in poetry would be like objecting to words there; for words, too, are symbols without the sensuous character of the things they stand for; and yet it is only by the net of new connections which words throw over things, in recalling them, that poetry arises at all. Poetry is an attenuation, a rehandling, an echo of crude experience; it is itself a theoretic vision of things at arm's length." *Ibid.*, p. 124.

124 V. *ibid.*, pp. 133–34.

125 V. *ibid.*, p. 212.

126 *Ibid.*, p. 213.

127 V. *ibid.*

128 "To play with nature and make it decorative, to play with the overtones of life and make them delightful, is a sort of art. It is the ultimate, the most artistic sort of art, but it will never be practised successfully so long as the other sort of art is in a backward state; for if we do not know our environment, we shall mistake our dreams for a part of it, and so spoil our science by making it fantastic, and our dreams by making them obligatory." *Ibid.*, p. 214.

CHAPTER IV

1 In *The Sense of Beauty* (1896); in *Interpretations of Poetry and Religion* (1900); and in "What Is Aesthetics?" (1904).

2 ". . . if we use the word life . . . to designate the happy maintenance against the world of some definite ideal interest, we may say . . . that life is reason in operation. The Life of Reason will then be a name for that part of experience which perceives and pursues ideals—all conduct so controlled and all sense so interpreted as to perfect natural happiness." *LR* I, 3.

3 "Reason . . . requires the fusion of two types of life, commonly led in the world in well-nigh total separation, one a life of impulse expressed in affairs and social passions, the other a life of reflection expressed in religion, science, and the imitative arts." *Ibid.*, p. 5.

4 "That brave humanity which had first raised its head in Hellas and had endowed so many things . . . with proportion and use, so that man's works might justify themselves to his mind, now found in Socrates its precise definition; and it was naturally where the Life of Reason had been long cultivated that it came finally to be conceived." *Ibid.*, p. 19.

5 "It was reserved for Plato to bring the Socratic ethics to its sublimest expression and to elicit from the depths of the Greek conscience those ancestral ideals which had inspired its legislators and had been embodied in its sacred civic traditions." *Ibid.*, p. 20.

6 "Beyond this point [viz., Plato's development of Socrates' ethics] no rendering of the Life of Reason has ever been carried. Aristotle improved the detail, and gave breadth and precision to many a part." *LR* I, 20. See also G. Santayana, *The Life of Reason,* V (New York, 1906), 240.

7 *Ibid.*, p. 21.

8 "The Life of Reason is . . . neither a mere means nor a mere incident in human progress; it is the total and embodied progress itself. . . ." *Ibid.*, p. 4.

9 "Reason and humanity begin with the union of instinct and ideation. . . ." *Ibid.*, p. 5.

10 "The Life of Reason is the happy marriage of two elements—impulse and ideation—which if wholly divorced would reduce man to a brute or to a maniac. The rational animal is generated by the union of these two monsters." *Ibid.*, p. 6.

11 "The problem is to unite a trustworthy conception of the conditions under which man lives with an adequate conception of his interests." *Ibid.*, p. 28.

[12] "The entire history of progress is a moral drama, a tale man might unfold in a great autobiography. . . ." *Ibid.*, p. 1.

[13] V. *ibid.*, p. 2.

[14] V. *ibid.*

[15] V. *ibid.*, pp. 2–3.

[16] "To increase . . . pleasures and reduce . . . pains would be to introduce an improvement into the sentient world, as if a devil suddenly died in hell or in heaven a new angel were created." *Ibid.*, p. 3.

[17] V. *ibid.*, pp. 3–4.

[18] "Reason and humanity begin . . . when instinct becomes enlightened, establishes values in its objects, and is *turned from a process into an art*, while at the same time consciousness becomes practical and cognitive, beginning to contain some symbol or record of the coordinate realities among which it arises." *Ibid.*, p. 5.

[19] ". . . the Life of Reason is another name for what . . . might be called Art." *Ibid.*, p. 6.

[20] V. *ibid.*

[21] V. *ibid.*

[22] V. *ibid.*, p. 7.

[23] V. *ibid.*

[24] V. *ibid.*

[25] "Every genuine ideal has a natural basis; anyone may understand and safely interpret it who is attentive to the life from which it springs." *Ibid.*, pp. 7–8.

[26] V. *ibid.*, p. 8.

[27] "Man . . . not only needs plasticity in his habits and pursuits but finds plasticity also in the surrounding world." *LR* IV, 3.

[28] Elsewhere Santayana explicitly affirms his compatibility with Spencer: "On the whole . . . I belong to Herbert Spencer's camp. . . . it seems evident to me that this world is the sort of world described by Herbert Spencer, not the sort of world described by Hegel or Bergson." *OS*, pp. 162–63.

[29] "Life is an equilibrium which is maintained now by accepting modification and now by imposing it." *LR* IV, 3.

[30] "Sometimes . . . man's traces are traces of useful action which has so changed natural objects as to make them congenial to his mind. . . . Any operation which thus humanises and rationalises objects is called art." *Ibid.*, p. 4.

[31] "All art has an instinctive source and a material embodiment." *Ibid.*

[32] "If the birds in building nests felt the utility of what they do, they would be practising an art; and for the instinct to be called rational it would even suffice that their traditional purpose and method should become conscious occasionally. Thus weaving is an art, although the weaver may not be at every moment conscious of its purpose, but may be carried along . . . by the routine of his art. . . ." *Ibid.*

[33] V. *ibid.*, p. 5.

[34] ". . . only by virtue of a false perspective do ideas seem to govern action, or is a felt necessity the mother of invention. In truth invention is the child of abundance, and the genius or vital premonition and groping which achieve art, simultaneously achieve the ideas which that art embodies; or, rather, ideas are themselves products of an inner movement which has an automatic extension outwards." *Ibid.*, p. 6.

[35] V. *ibid.*

[36] "Arts are instincts bred and reared in the open, creative habits acquired in the light of reason." *Ibid.*, p. 5.

[37] V. *ibid.*, p. 7.

38 "The most useful act will never be repeated unless its secret remains embodied in structure." *Ibid.*, p. 10.

39 *V. ibid.*

40 *Ibid.*, p. 11.

41 "What makes progress possible is that rational action may leave traces in nature, such that nature in consequence furnishes a better basis for the Life of Reason; in other words progress is art bettering the conditions of existence." *Ibid.*, p. 13.

42 "Art, in establishing instruments for human life beyond the human body, and moulding outer things into sympathy with inner values, establishes a ground whence values may continually spring up." *Ibid.*

43 *V. ibid.*

44 *V. ibid.*, p. 15.

45 *V. ibid.*, pp. 14–15.

46 "If art is that element in the Life of Reason which consists in modifying its environment the better to attain its end, art may be expected to subserve all parts of the human ideal, to increase man's comfort, knowledge, and delight. And as nature . . . is wont to satisfy these interests together, so art, in seeking to increase that satisfaction, will work simultaneously in every ideal direction." *Ibid.*, pp. 16–17.

47 Cf. J. Ashmore, "Santayana's Mistrust of Fine Art," *The Journal of Aesthetics and Art Criticism,* 14 (March, 1956), 339–47.

48 "The values inherent in imagination . . . are called aesthetic values; they are found mainly in nature and living beings, but often also in man's artificial works, in images evoked by language, and in the realm of sound." *LR IV,* 15.

49 *V. ibid.*, p. 16.

50 "To separate the aesthetic element . . . is an artifice which is more misleading than helpful; for neither in the history of art nor in a rational estimate of its value can the aesthetic function of things be divorced from the practical and moral." *Ibid.*

51 "An aesthetic fragrance, indeed, all things may have, if in soliciting man's senses or reason they can awaken his imagination as well, but this middle zone . . . cannot well be treated in theory otherwise than as . . . a phase of man's sympathy with the world he moves in." *Ibid.*

52 ". . . life . . . is initially experimental and . . . experiment fortifies certain tendencies and cancels others, so that a gradual sediment of habit and wisdom is formed in the stream of time. Action then ceases to be merely tentative and spontaneous, and becomes art." *Ibid.*, p. 35.

53 *V. ibid.*, pp. 36–37.

54 *V. ibid.*, pp. 35–36.

55 ". . . utility leads to art when its vehicle acquires intrinsic value and becomes expressive. . . . spontaneous action leads to art when it acquires a rational function." *Ibid.*, p. 36.

56 *Ibid.*

57 ". . . the fine arts . . . grow, now out of utility, now out of automatism. . . . their goal . . . can be nothing but the complete superposition of these two characters." *Ibid.*, pp. 36–37.

58 *V. ibid.*, p. 37.

59 *V. ibid.*

60 *V. ibid.*, pp. 37–38.

61 *V. ibid.*, p. 39.

62 "The automatic performer, being . . . controlled more or less by reflection and criticism, becomes something of an artist: he trains himself to be consecutive, impressive, agreeable; he begins to compare his improvisation with

its subject and function, and thus he develops what is called style and taste."
Ibid., p. 43.

63 ". . . all industry contains an element of fine art and all fine art an element of industry. . . ." *Ibid.*, p. 33.

64 ". . . fine arts are seldom an original factor in human progress. . . ." *Ibid.*, p. 217.

65 "Art . . . is one more source of unhappiness . . . so long as it is not squared with . . . necessary labors and merely interrupts them [as most fine art does]." *Ibid.*, p. 220.

66 ". . . all art, like the whole Life of Reason, is joined together at its roots, and branches out from the vital processes of sensation and reaction. Diversity arises centrifugally, according to the provinces explored. . . ." *Ibid.*, p. 164.

67 V. *ibid.*, pp. 44–45.

68 V. *ibid.*, pp. 46–47.

69 V. *ibid.*, p. 68.

70 V. *ibid.*, pp. 87–88.

71 "Sometimes, in impressing the environment, a man will improve it. . . . As soon as this . . . is perceived and the act is done with knowledge of its ensuing benefits, plastic impulse becomes art, and the world begins actually to change in obedience to reason." *Ibid.*, p. 118.

72 "One respect . . . in which man depends on things is for the aesthetic quality of his perceptions. If he happens, by a twist of the hand, to turn a flowering branch into a wreath, thereby making it more interesting, he will have discovered a decorative art. . . ." *Ibid.*, pp. 118–19.

73 V. *ibid.*, p. 119.

74 V. *ibid.*, p. 52.

75 V. *ibid.*, p. 90.

76 V. *ibid.*, p. 127.

77 V. *ibid.*, p. 144.

78 V. *ibid.*

79 V. *ibid.*, pp. 145–46.

80 V. *ibid.*, p. 147.

81 Santayana uses the example of shipbuilding: "The rationality of shipbuilding has several sets of conditions: . . . the patron's specifications have to be judged by the purpose he in turn has in mind; this purpose itself has to be justified by his ideal in life, and finally his ideal by its adequacy to his total or ultimate nature. Error on any of these planes makes the ultimate product irrational. . . ." *Ibid.*, pp. 18–19.

82 V. *ibid.*, p. 21.

83 V. *ibid.*

84 V. *ibid.*, pp. 21–22.

85 ". . . rationality does not accrue to spirit because mechanism supports it; it accrues to mechanism insofar as spirit is thereby called into existence; so that while values derive existence only from their causes, causes derive value only from their results." *Ibid.*, p. 22.

86 "A man . . . must be credited with some rational capacity: prospect and retrospect, hope and the ideal portraiture of things, must to some extent employ him." *Ibid.*, p. 24.

87 "The ideal is a concomitant emanation from the natural and has no other possible status." *Ibid.*, p. 28.

88 "All objects envisaged either in vulgar action or in the airiest cognition must be at first ideal and distinct from the given facts, otherwise action would have lost its function at the same moment that thought lost its significance." *Ibid.*, p. 29.

89 V. *ibid.*, pp. 29–30.

90 "Art . . . has two stages: one mechanical or industrial, in which untoward matter is better prepared, or impeding media are overcome; the other liberal, in which perfectly fit matter is appropriated to ideal uses and endowed with a direct spiritual function." *Ibid.*, p. 32.

91 "A certain amount of technical and instrumental labor is involved in every work of genius, and a certain genius in every technical success." *Ibid.*, p. 33.

92 ". . . the fine arts are seldom an original factor in human progress. If they express moral and political greatness, and serve to enhance it, they acquire a certain dignity; but so soon as this expressive function is abandoned they grow meretricious." *Ibid.*, p. 217.

93 "Never have art and beauty received a more glowing eulogy than is implied in Plato's censure. . . . This was done in the ultimate interest of art and beauty, which in a cultivated mind are inseparable from the vitally good." *Ibid.*, p. 177.

94 "It is mere barbarism to feel that a thing is aesthetically good but morally evil, or morally good but hateful to perception." *Ibid.*, p. 177.

95 V. *ibid.*, p. 94.

96 "Any absolute work of art which serves no further purpose than to stimulate an emotion has about it a certain luxurious and visionary taint. . . . Art, so long as it needs to be a dream, will never cease to prove a disappointment. . . . In the mere artist, too, there is always something that falls short of the gentleman and that defeats the man." *Ibid.*, pp. 211–12.

97 "To exalt fine art into a truly ideal activity we should have to knit it more closely with other rational functions, so that to beautify things might render them more useful and to represent them most imaginatively might be to see them in their truth. Something of the sort has been actually attained by the noblest arts in their noblest phases." *Ibid.*, p. 213.

98 "The joys of creating are not confined . . . to those who create things without practical uses. . . . Architecture may be useful, sculpture commemorative, poetry reflective, even music, by its expression, religious or martial. In a word, practical exigencies, in calling forth the arts, give them moral functions which it is a pleasure to see them fulfill." *Ibid.*, p. 210.

99 V. *ibid.*, pp. 212–13.

100 Santayana invites confusion in the interpretation of the terms, art and fine art. Ordinarily the term, art, includes the extension of the term, fine art; but in Santayana's writing it almost never does. In his distinctive usage, art almost always denotes activity pursued in conformity with a rational ideal, and fine art is largely excluded from this province. In the interest of intelligibility this study has adopted the convention of signifying rational art wherever the term, art, is used alone, and when the denotation happens to be fine art that term is given without ellipsis. In this way Santayana's own usage is followed throughout.

101 "Moral harmonies . . . are not given; they have to be made." *Ibid.*, p. 166.

102 "The function of ethics is precisely . . . to fix the ultimate resultant of all given interests insofar as they can be combined. . . . wisdom consists in knowing what goods to sacrifice and what simples to pour into the supreme mixture." *Ibid.*, p. 167.

103 V. *ibid.*

104 "It is in the world . . . that art must find its level. It must vindicate its function in the human commonwealth." *Ibid.*, p. 168.

105 "Now [fine] art, more than any other considerable pursuit, . . . is abstract and inconsequential. Born of suspended attention, it ends in itself." *Ibid.*, p. 170.

106 ". . . [fine] art registers passions without stimulating them; . . . in stopping to depict them it steals away their life; and whatever interest and delight it transfers to their expression it subtracts from their vital energy." *Ibid.*

107 "They [the arts] give as nature does, a form to matter, but they give it a more propitious form." *Ibid.*, p. 32.

108 "In aesthetic activity we have . . . one side of rational life; sensuous experience is dominated there as mechanical or social realities ought to be dominated in science and politics." *Ibid.*, p. 171.

109 ". . . art in general is a rehearsal of rational living, and recasts in idea a world which we have no present means of recasting in reality. Yet this rehearsal reveals the glories of a possible performance better than do the miserable experiments until now executed on the reality." *Ibid.*, pp. 172–73.

110 "What nature does with existence, art does with appearance; and while the achievement leaves us, unhappily, much where we were before in all our efficacious relations, it entirely renews our vision and breeds a fresh world in fancy, where all form has the same inner justification that all life has in the real world." *Ibid.*, pp. 173–74. Santayana's use of the term, art, sometimes is confusing. In this passage he seems to denote fine art to the exclusion of rational art, and to grant merit to fine art, which is counter to his usual view.

111 V. *ibid.*, p. 179.

112 ". . . in truth material life itself would be nothing worth, were it not, in its essence and its issue, ideal." *Ibid.*

113 "In educating the imagination art crowns all moral endeavour, which from the beginning is a species of art, and which becomes a fine art more completely as it works in a freer medium." *Ibid.*, p. 181.

114 V. *ibid.*

115 "Aesthetic sensibility colors every thought, qualifies every allegiance, and modifies every product of human labor. Consequently the love of beauty has to justify itself not merely intrinsically, or as a constituent part of life more or less to be insisted upon; it has to justify itself also as an influence." *Ibid.*, p. 183.

116 ". . . aesthetic and other interests are not separable units, to be compared externally; they are rather strands interwoven in the texture of everything." *Ibid.*

117 Again Santayana is equivocal in his use of the term, art. Surely fine art is supreme in organization of sensuous elements and, in such a context, the term, art, when Santayana uses it without qualification, will be construed as designating fine art.

118 V. *ibid.*, p. 184.

119 V. *ibid.*, p. 185.

120 V. *ibid.*, p. 186. In this passage the reference to art may include more than fine art, since the condition of utility is mentioned. Precise interpretation of "art" in this and several other passages seems baffling.

121 "Aesthetic values everywhere precede and accompany rational activity, and life is, in one aspect, always a fine art. . . . an aesthetic sanction sweetens all successful living; animal efficiency cannot be without grace, nor moral achievement without a sensible glory." *Ibid.*, p. 188.

122 V. *ibid.*

123 ". . . of all premature settlements the most premature is that which the fine arts are wont to establish. A harmony in appearance only, one that touches the springs of nothing and has no power to propagate itself, is so partial a good that we may justly call it an illusion." *Ibid.*, p. 216.

124 ". . . aesthetic harmony, so incomplete in its basis as to be fleeting and deceptive, is most complete in its form. This so partial synthesis is a synthesis

indeed, and just because settlements made in fancy are altogether premature, and ignore almost everything in the world, in type they can be the most perfect settlements." *Ibid.*, p. 218.

125 V. *ibid.*, p. 219.

126 V. *ibid.*, p. 220.

127 V. *ibid.*, pp. 221–22.

128 "The principle that all institutions should subserve happiness runs deeper than any cult for art and lays the foundation on which the latter might rest safely. If social structure were rational its free expression would be so too." *Ibid.*, p. 224.

129 Here it seems Santayana is referring to all kinds of art.

130 V. *ibid.*, p. 229.

131 "In industry man is still servile, preparing the materials he is to use in action. In action itself, though he is free, he exerts his influence on a living and treacherous medium and sees the issue at each moment drift farther and farther from his intent. In science he is an observer, preparing himself for action in another way, by studying its results and conditions. But in art he is at once competent and free, he is creative." *Ibid.*

CHAPTER V

1 *The Dial*, 73 (July, 1922), 25–31. Reprinted in *Obiter Scripta*. Subsequent references are to *Obiter Scripta*.

2 *The Dial*, 82 (May, 1927), 361–70. Reprinted in *Obiter Scripta*. Subsequent references are to *Obiter Scripta*.

3 *The Philosophical Review*, 34 (May, 1925), 281–91.

4 New York.

5 Quite some portion of *Dominations and Powers* is a rewriting of long standing notes: "The thought of seeing history in the terms of Dominations and Powers came to me soon after I had completed writing *The Life of Reason*. Before the war of 1914–1918 I had set down various paragraphs or short essays on the subject. . . . I soon busied myself with other things; yet sometimes a philosophical argument would ramble into reflections which, on revision, I would take out and put aside under the title of *Dominations and Powers*." *DP*, p. 22.

6 "Many years ago . . . I drew a sketch of human society inspired by the ethics of Plato and Aristotle. . . . If I now submit . . . some subsequent thoughts on the same subject, I do so with a more modest intention. I have become aware that anyone's sense of what is good and beautiful must have a somewhat narrow foundation, namely, his circumstances and his particular brand of human nature; and he should not expect the good or the beautiful after his own heart to be greatly prevalent or long maintained in the world." *Ibid.*, p. vii.

7 *OS*, p. 153.

8 ". . . somebody must still manufacture official statues and family portraits, somebody must design apartment houses, clubs, churches, skyscrapers, and stations. Visible through the academic framework of these inevitable objects, there is often much professional learning. . . . Taste of the old honest worldly sort is far from dead; it is found still in milliners and designers of fashionable garments, of furniture and ornaments. All this luxurious traditional art is as far as possible from repentance." *Ibid.*, p. 152.

9 V. *ibid.*, pp. 153–54.

10 "I call pure color and caricature penitent art, because it is only disappointment in other directions that drives artists back to these primary effects. By an

austere and deliberate abstinence from everything that naturally tempts them, they achieve in this way a certain peace; but they would far rather have found it by genuinely recovering their naivete." *Ibid.,* p. 153.

11 *V. ibid.,* p. 155. Here Santayana mentions cubism as an example of his point.

12 *Ibid.,* p. 157.

13 *Ibid.,* p. 156.

14 *Ibid.*

15 *V. ibid.,* pp. 156–57.

16 *V. ibid.,* p. 157.

17 *V. ibid.,* p. 158. It seems almost certain that the painting of Klee and Miró is the basis for Santayana's remarks about penitent caricature.

18 "Do not make maps of your images; . . . Be reticent, emphatic, moody, bold; *salvation lies in caricature." Ibid.*

19 "Savages were never rudimentary on purpose; they were not experimenting in the distortion or simplification of forms; much less . . . did they voluntarily eliminate all representation of objects in order to deepen sensibility for the medium. They simply painted as well as they could." *Ibid.*

20 *V. ibid.*

21 *V. ibid.,* p. 159.

22 *V. ibid.*

23 *V. ibid.*

24 "These images [represented in penitent caricature] are not the forms of things at all . . . their character . . . is amazingly summary, variable, and fantastic—a mere wraith, a mere hint, a mere symbol." *Ibid.,* p. 160.

25 *Ibid.*

26 *V. ibid.*

27 *V. ibid.,* pp. 160–61.

28 "Whenever a Soviet . . . would impose its authority by force or by eloquent dogmas, it evidently forfeits the spiritual spontaneity which I am assigning to it." *Ibid.,* p. 250.

29 ". . . the aesthete is a sort of intellectual voluptuary who thinks that everything is made . . . simply for his contemplative satisfaction. And the aesthetic soul in the artists themselves takes this view, especially in musicians and painters, whose work has no immediate practical function. . . . they may proclaim the independence of the spiritual quality, the free imaginative element, in their works; this . . . makes the true professional link between them . . . and in its name they may well establish an aesthetic Soviet." *Ibid.,* pp. 252–53.

30 ". . . the field of the aesthetically obvious is infinitely extensible: every caprice or marvel of form, natural or unnatural, is waiting in the limbo of essence for the hand or the eye that shall bring it to light." *Ibid.,* p. 251.

31 *V. ibid.,* pp. 250–51.

32 The distinction suggested between artist and "fine artist" has immense significance within the writings of Santayana. The same distinction is not made in common parlance.

33 "Artists are craftsmen working under the patronage of industry, religion, custom, sentiment, or pride. They are not aesthetes. . . ." *Ibid.,* p. 252.

34 ". . . if they [artists] are to excel in their crafts they must have a good eye and a deft hand. . . ." *Ibid.*

35 *V. ibid.,* pp. 251–53.

36 "The chief difficulties which might beset a Soviet . . . even of artistic craftsmen, are vain and harmless in the impalpable realms of intuition." *Ibid.,* p. 253.

37 "As sight requires a lens to focus and redistribute the interfused rays of

light, so government requires a governor in whose brain and heart all interests may be synthesized and all actions co-ordinated. But for intuition the only lens needed is that which nature creates in each living organism. . . ." *Ibid.*

38 V. *ibid.*, pp. 254–55.

39 "The truth and beauty which we profess to love would leave us profoundly disconsolate, if we could not dance before them holding hands and assuring ourselves, by saying so in chorus, that this beauty is really beautiful and this truth really true." *Ibid.*, pp. 255–56.

40 V. *ibid.*, p. 257.

41 V. *ibid.*, p. 256.

42 "A construction in colors does not contradict or verify a construction in sounds; nor would a tragedy contradict a comedy, or another tragedy . . . unless these various essences were understood to describe the same series of events, stumblingly enacted or brutally endured by living animals, and not in the least created by the intuition. . . ." *Ibid.*, pp. 257–58.

43 "All nature is one great institution, of which animal bodies and human customs are in their day constituent parts: the freest spirit alive is a cub in that litter." *Ibid.*, p. 258.

44 V. *ibid.*

45 V. *ibid.*, p. 260.

46 *Ibid.*

47 V. *ibid.*, p. 261.

48 V. *ibid.*, pp. 260–61.

49 *Ibid.*, p. 262.

50 V. *ibid.*

51 V. *ibid.*, pp. 262–63.

52 "We must expect the arts to remain in the hands of traditional artists; but these artists will lose nothing by occasionally joining an aesthetic Soviet for a sort of holiday or carnival. They will return to their workshops greatly refreshed. . . ." *Ibid.*, p. 263.

53 *Ibid.*, p. 264.

54 New York, 1924.

55 Cf. above, pp. 39–43.

56 V. *MAC*, p. 281.

57 V. *ibid.*

58 V. *ibid.*

59 ". . . the Useful exercises an indirect control over the Moral Good . . . and since the Beautiful is defined . . . to be 'that which yields a relatively permanent or stable field of pleasure,' the Useful will be a subsidiary part of the Beautiful. Thus, in spite of the alleged separation of the Beautiful from the Moral Good, even the Moral Good, since it is controlled by utility, turns out to be subterraneously dependent for its continued authority on the beauties which the recognition of it will eventually produce." *Ibid.*, p. 283.

60 *Ibid.*, p. 282.

61 V. *ibid.*

62 "Among the Greeks the idea of happiness was aesthetic and that of beauty moral; and this not because the Greeks were confused but because they were civilized." *Ibid.*

63 V. *ibid.*, pp. 283–84.

64 *Ibid.*, p. 284.

65 V. *ibid.*, p. 285.

66 V. *ibid.*

67 *Ibid.*, p. 286.

68 And he continues: "They [i.e., antecedents and conditions] are ideas

which thought creates when it needs them, not genuine antecedents which create thought." *Ibid.*, p. 285.

69 *V. ibid.*, p. 286.

70 ". . . the value which the romanticist finds in life or in beauty is that of a vent for something lower; and although . . . he may deny that such a nether power exists, yet he always looks upon overt appearance as on something forged by his own lurid efforts, as if the very devil had been in him." *Ibid.*

71 *V. ibid.*

72 *V. ibid.*

73 ". . . every idea, after being inflated by his [the romanticist's] thought, collapses at once into a husk and a dead form to him, as his spirit hastens on to some fresh embodiment." *Ibid.*

74 *Ibid.*

75 *V. ibid.*

76 *Ibid.*, p. 287.

77 *V. ibid.*

78 *V. ibid.*

79 *Ibid.*

80 *Ibid.*

81 *Ibid.*, p. 288.

82 *V. ibid.*

83 "There are portentous works, like those of Michelangelo or Tintoretto, to which every one will assign a high rank . . . but the interest and wonder which they arouse may rarely . . . pass into a true glimpse of the beautiful." *Ibid.*

84 "It is not beauty that collectors or connoisseurs look for in the arts. The more a poet or a psychologist insists on the thrilling and seductive note which to him is the soul of the beautiful, the less will his theory of beauty be a theory of art; his sensibility will not help him to understand the arts or even to enjoy them." *Ibid.*

85 *V. ibid.*

86 ". . . I think a lover of beauty will soon turn his back on concert-halls and museums, and take to the fields." *Ibid.*

87 *LR* IV, 129. In *Dominations and Powers* Santayana reconfirms the point: "A genuine lover of the beautiful would never enter a museum." *DP*, p. 277.

88 *MAC*, p. 289.

89 *V. ibid.*

90 ". . . I suppose that the first line of a poem, or the new or peculiar characters of any design, must occur to the mind unbidden before the artist, in his capacity of expert workman and critic, can plan his work as a whole and laboriously execute it." *Ibid.*

91 *Ibid.*

92 *V. ibid.*

93 "I am far from wishing to imply that . . . generations of faithful and genial artists had no love for the beautiful. . . ." *Ibid.*, p. 290.

94 ". . . they [artists] saw it [the beautiful] in nature, in the model; and it was because they loved it so intensely . . . in nature that they wished to transfer it to their works with as little loss as possible of its vital power." *Ibid.*

95 *Ibid.*, p. 291.

CHAPTER VI

Section 1 of this chapter is a revised version of the author's paper, "Santayana's Qualification of Objectified Pleasure," presented at the XIII International Congress of Philosophy, Mexico D.F., Mexico, September 7–14, 1963.

1 *MAC*, 284n.
2 *Ibid.*
3 V. *ibid.*
4 *Ibid.*
5 *Ibid.*
6 *RB*, p. 8.
7 *Ibid.*
8 *Ibid.*, pp. 152–53.
9 *Ibid.*, p. 152.
10 "Intuition is liberating on every level. . . . from passion it liberates eloquence, poetry and beauty. . . ." *Ibid.*, pp. 523–24.
11 V. *ibid.*, pp. 7–8.
12 *The Journal of Philosophy*, 18 (December 22, 1921), 701–13. Reprinted in *SELS*, from which subsequent citations are taken.
13 *SELS*, pp. 247–48.
14 *Ibid.*, p. 250.
15 V. *ibid.*, p. 254.
16 *Ibid.*
17 *Ibid.*
18 *Ibid.*
19 *Ibid.*, p. 255.
20 V. *ibid.*, p. 249.
21 V. *ibid.*
22 V. *DP*, p. vii.
23 V. *ibid.*
24 "Neither historical investigation . . . nor political precepts are to be looked for in this book [*Dominations and Powers*]. All that it professes to contain is glimpses of tragedy and comedy played unawares by governments. . . ." *Ibid.*, p. ix.
25 *Ibid.*, p. 23.
26 *Ibid.*, p. 24.
27 *Ibid.*, p. 25.
28 *LR* I, 21.
29 *DP*, p. 2.
30 *Ibid.*, p. 26.
31 The distinctions between generative, militant, and rational orders, and the distinction between dominations and powers "are not to be taken for *separate natural processes,* such as history or natural science might distinguish . . . all events arise according to the Generative Order of Nature, whether by involuntary growth or militant action or rational action. . . . The distinctions are made *not in view of any distinct forces* imagined to be at work in the world, *but in view of the different moral results* generated by the concourse of all natural forces." *Ibid.*, p. 177.
32 *Ibid.*, p. 26.
33 "All dominations involve an exercise of power, but . . . not all Powers are Dominations." *Ibid.*, p. 1.
34 *Ibid.*
35 V. *ibid.*
36 V. *ibid.*
37 ". . . unless it be in the Garden of Eden, people require clothes and shelter, and furniture of many kinds." *Ibid.*, p. 25.
38 V. *ibid.*
39 "Trades must . . . be allowed to exist, at least in the service of rustic life and in its defence." *Ibid.*

40 V. *ibid.*

41 ". . . all events arise according to the Generative Order of Nature, whether by involuntary growth or by militant or rational action. . . ." *Ibid.,* p. 177.

42 V. *ibid.*

43 *Ibid.,* p. 91.

44 ". . . the greater and swifter the power that mechanical instruments put in man's hands, the greater will be the occasional temptation that will assail him to put this power to the test. And this is socially and morally an omnipotent power, less to produce than to destroy. . . ." *Ibid.,* p. 89.

45 "All arts are powers in danger of becoming dominations because, necessarily having organs in the psyche and many of them also instruments in the public world, they are rivals, and each tends to monopolise the energies of life at the expense of other developments or even at the price of life itself." *Ibid.,* p. 94.

46 V. *ibid.,* p. 92.

47 "Agriculture . . . excites the feeling of proprietorship with a particular force. It is not only his present property that a wicked enemy threatens to rob the farmer of, but of his father's heritage, of his whole future and of that of his children. . . .

"This intense proprietary passion repeats in a human form the absolute fury with which the bulldog clings to whatever he holds in his teeth. The same feeling, variously qualified, animates all economic art." *Ibid.,* pp. 92–93.

48 "Economic arts in particular . . . deviate in all directions from rational industry, run into the opposite blind alleys of avarice and luxury, and equip militant egotism with instruments for its mad experiments. All this occurs because the motive force in economic labor always remains some offshoot of primitive greed and cupidity. The good to be attained is not seen or imagined; there is at bottom only an indiscriminate impulse to grasp, to keep, and to swallow." *Ibid.,* p. 93.

49 V. *ibid.,* p. 94.

50 V. *ibid.,* p. 340.

51 V. *ibid.,* p. 98.

52 V. *ibid.,* pp. 120–21.

53 *Ibid.,* pp. 89, 93.

54 "As arts they [manual and ideal arts] cannot conflict; it is only the persons that practice them that may be rivals for place or reputation in society, and the more so when the art they practice is the same and in the same country. . . ." *Ibid.,* p. 121.

55 V. *ibid.,* p. 107.

56 "Monarchy is government by a single psyche, by the organizing principle of a living soul. Organization signifies the cooperative regimen of a great variety of functions, senses, and instruments. It makes possible, by properly timing and spacing those different activities, to make room, without disorder or conflict, for the most various types of life." *Ibid.,* p. 109.

57 V. *ibid.,* p. 110.

58 "Liberal arts are relevant to government only as the whole realm of spirit is relevant to physical life, by witnessing it and supplying it with a moral excuse for being." *Ibid.,* p. 141.

59 *Ibid.,* p. 152.

60 "It [music] is . . . a signal proof of the unexpected fertility of the generative order in the liberal dimensions; for all this science, all this art, all this unfeigned pleasure and exaltation, comes to us, as it were, from nowhere,

serves us for nothing ulterior, and yet seems to us the elixir and finest flower of the spirit." *Ibid.*, p. 139.

61 ". . . the movement [of music] must beat time to specific cosmical rhythms. The horizons of music are all its own, boundless, free, ultrahuman. . . ." *Ibid.*, pp. 138–39.

62 V. *ibid.*, p. 139.

63 ". . . industry, in its beginnings and in its vital impulse, had always been a spontaneous habit, even in some of the lower animals, when they possess bills, fingers, or can weave nets with fibres spun within their bodies, as in the case of birds, monkeys or kangaroos, and spiders. And in man this playful industry found many economic uses and at the same time developed a variety of liberal arts." *Ibid.*, p. 262.

64 V. *ibid.*, p. 168.

65 V. *ibid.*, pp. 168–69.

66 V. *ibid.*, p. 171.

67 V. *ibid.*, p. 329.

CHAPTER VII

1 V. SELS, p. 257.

2 PGS, p. 20.

3 *Ibid.*, p. 538.

4 *Ibid.*, p. 549.

5 *Ibid.*, p. 15.

6 *Ibid.*, pp. 9, 13.

7 V. MS, p. 7.

8 V. GS, p. 33.

9 T. Lipps, "Einfühlung, innere Nachahmung, und Organenempfindungen," *Archiv für die gesamte Psychologie*, I (1903), 185–204, tr. M. Schertel and M. Rader, in *A Modern Book of Esthetics* (New York, 1935), pp. 291–304. The passage quoted is on pp. 293–94. Italics are the translators'.

10 GS, p. 35.

11 SB, p. 97.

12 OS, pp. 162–63; also v. OS, pp. 165–66.

13 J. S. Mill, *Three Essays on Religion*, p. 103, quoted in GS.

14 Cf. above, 52–54.

15 G. Santayana, *My Host the World: Persons and Places*, III (New York, 1953), 153.

16 PP, 256.

17 MS, 152–53.

18 G. Santayana, "Three American Philosophers," *The American Scholar*, XXII (Summer, 1953), 284.

19 G. Santayana, "The Idler and His Works," *Saturday Review*, XXXVII (May 15, 1954), 48.

20 *Ibid.*, pp. 48–49.

21 D. Cory, *Santayana: The Later Years* (New York, 1963), p. 182.

Index

Aesthetic theory, viii, 52, 77. *See also* Aesthetics

Aestheticism, 74

Aesthetics: aesthetic quality, 40; paradox of, 40; and reasoned knowledge, 40; excluded from philosophy and psychology, 41; and moral idealism, 41; as part of the rational ideal, 42; as an equivocal term, 50; biological sources of, 51; ambiguity of the term, 78; mentioned, vii–ix, 1–14 *passim*, 25–26, 39, 52, 70–83 *passim*, 97–103 *passim*, 106n1,12, 14, 107n1, 110n51

Apperception: and indeterminate form, 18; distingiushed from description, 18; of form, 112n82; mentioned, 17

Apperceptive type: and aesthetic value, 19; mentioned, 17, 18, 20

Architecture: as fine art, 62; origin in plastic construction, 62; mentioned, 69, 106n12, 124n98

Aristotle, 3, 52–53, 90, 99, 120n6, 126n6

Arnett, Willard Eugene, vii–ix, 98

Arnold, Matthew, 26, 99–100, 114n3,4

Arrangement: economy of as expression, 22–23

Art: philosophy of, vii, 98, 106n1; objects of, 21; as imitation, 35; as interpretation, 35; according to nature, 35; according to rules, 35; and living, 51; rational, two modes of, 49; and the Life of Reason, 55, 121n19; two factors in, 56; and utility, 56–57, 121n32, 122n55; transmission of, 57; and instinct, 57, 121n36; and structure, 58; distinguished from fine art, 58–60, 69, 124n100; effect on environment, 58, 64; satisfactions of, 58; liberal, 59, 64, 69, 124n90; as servile, 59; as ranked by automatism and utility, 60; origin same as fine art, 61; and mechanical procedure, 63; two conditions for rationality, 63; mechanical, 64, 69, 124n90; stages of, 64, 96, 124n90; and material, 65; and education, 66; and experience, 66; and imagination, 66, 125n113; and the state, 66; and nature, 66–67, 125n107; and life, 67; of life, 67, 95, 114n18; and freedom, 68, 126n131; and happiness, 68; and institutions, 68; genesis and development, 68; scope of the term, 68; pre-rational, 69; and environment,

69; penitent, 71, 126*n10;* penitent, kinds of, 72; penitent, criticism of, 73; dependence on technique, 81–82; parasitical, 91; as necessary and as optional, 92; mechanical and industrial, 93; economic distinguished from liberal, 93, 102; and passion, 94; and greed, 94; liberal and industrial, 94–95, 132*n63;* of government, 95; useful and liberal, 96; and play, 96; Greek, 114*n3;* as play with nature, 120*n128;* imitative, 120*n3;* and objects, 121*n30;* history and value of, 122*n50;* and progress, 122*n41;* and action, 122*n55;* and impulse, 123*n71;* discovery of, 123*n72;* and appearance, 125*n110;* and moral endeavor, 125*n113;* traditional, 126*n8;* and tradition, 128*n52;* and collectors, 129*n84;* as power, 131*n45;* economic, 131*n47,48;* economic and greed, 131*n48;* manual and ideal, 131*n54;* liberal, and government, 131*n58;* mentioned, vii, ix, 1–9 *passim,* 19–26 *passim,* 39–52 *passim,* 61–74 *passim,* 83, 90–103 *passim,* 106*n,* 108*n21,* 113*n116,* 114*n4,* 116*n43,* 121*n31,34,* 122*n42,* 46,52, 123*n65,66,* 124*n93,96,104,* 125*n109,117,120,* 126*n128,* 131*n60.* *See also* Fine Art

Artist: two senses of the term, 75; as craftsmen, 127*n33,34,36;* as workmen, 129*n90;* and love of the beautiful, 129*n93,94;* and nature, 129*n94;* mentioned, 74

Association: in euphuism, 31

Automatism: of nature, 101; and fine art, 122*n57;* mentioned, 60–61. *See also* Spontaneity

Avila, 3

Beautiful, the: categorial ambiguity, 78; mentioned, 79, 128*n59*

Beauty: perception of, 8; as desire, 9; and pleasure, 9, 11–12, 83, 85–86; experience of, 9; as independent of eternal form, 11; as independent of objects, 11; as relative, 11; and expression, 12, 23; and form, 12, 14–15, 17, 20, 24, 83, 110*n61,* 111*n53;* and material, 12–13, 83,

110*n,* 111*n54,* 112*n74;* influence of passion of love, 12; influence of sexual instinct, 12, 109*n32;* influence of social instincts, 12; sensuous, 13–14; sense of, 14, 21, 24, 32, 39, 81, 85, 88, 97, 101, 113*n105;* from multiplicity in uniformity, 17; and indeterminate form, 18–19; from expression, 22; and form in tragedy, 23; illusion of its objectivity, 23; described, 23–24; and poetry, 31, 38; criterion for, 37; material of, in poetry, 37; as ineradicable, 43, 50; as a unifying principle, 50; and value, 51; derivation, 75; for the Greeks, 78, 128*n62;* as related to fine art, 81–82; Marshall's doctrine of, 81; as essence, 85–88; as vital harmony, 85–88; material, formal, and expressive conditions of, 86–87; properties of, 87; visionary and indefinable, 87; psychology of, 98; of science and mathematics, 116*n44;* principle of, 116*n48;* love of, 125*n115;* and collectors, 129*n84;* mentioned, viii–ix, 2–3, 10, 13, 42, 59–65 *passim,* 70, 76–86 *passim,* 90, 103, 108*n,* 109*n28,* 110*n39,* 113*n102,* 117*n66,* 124*n93,* 128*n39,* 129*n70,86*

Bergson, Henri, 121*n28*

Blanshard, Brand, 3

Bosanquet, Bernard, 79–80

Boston, 3

Consciousness: and value, 7; emotional, 108*n19;* tone of, 113*n115;* mentioned, 8–10, 13, 23, 39, 73, 111*n69,* 113*n107,* 119*n112,* 121*n18*

Cost: as expression, 22–23; mentioned, 113*n115*

Criticism: theories of, 26; aesthetic, 27, 39, 44, 119*n115;* of poetry, 30, 43, 45, 52, 70; and moral philosophy, 42; categories of reference, 42; of penitent art, 73; German, 117*n65;* mentioned, 6

Croce, Benedetto, 78–80

Dante, 44, 46, 48, 50, 119*n122*

Democritus, 3

Desire, 5, 8–9, 11, 13, 36, 53, 93. *See also* Interest; Will

Dewey, John, vii, 103
Dominations: distinguished from powers, 92, 130n31,33; mentioned, 91, 102

Ebbinghaus, Hermann, 3, 26, 99–100
Emotion: and value, 13; from sensing of multiplicity and continuity, 16; of pleasure, 22; and poetry, 32–34, 47, 115n35,36,38, 119n116; and philosophy, 47–48; mentioned, 9, 17, 22, 85, 89, 109n29, 114n3, 116n47,48,53, 117n65, 119n118, 124n96. See also Passion
Empedocles: doctrine of, 37
Epistemology, vii–viii
Essence: contemplation of, 6; doctrine of, 85; intuition of, 106n2; mentioned, 84, 86–87, 113n2, 127n30, 128n42
Ethics, 52, 65. See also Philosophy, moral
Euphony, 31
Euphuism, 31
Existence, vii
Experience: human, vii–ix, 4–5, 40–41, 66, 89; contemplative, viii; aesthetic, 1, 4, 9–10, 12, 26–27, 40, 43, 51, 97–99; of value, 9–11, 83; of pleasure, 11; of outer objects, 13; in apperception, 19; of determinate form, 20; and association, 21–22; and tragedy, 23; sense, 29, 67, 74, 90; emotional, 31, 50; layers of, 31; perceptual, 32; and common sense, 33; and poetry, 33–34, 120n123; actual, 80; of discourse, 84; subjectivity of, 84; natural, 91; material of, 116n42,43; of good and evil, 117n69; sensuous, 125n106; mentioned, 32, 46–47, 52–53, 79, 90, 100, 102, 106n7, 109n36, 111n69, 113n107, 114n21, 115n23, 34, 116n47, 117n60, 120n2
Expression: based on association, 21; as internal to the mind, 22; compared with material and formal value, 22; expressive thing, 22; theory of, 22; and tragedy, 23; emotional contrasted with intellectual, 31; imaginative, 35; sensuous, 35; poetic compared with philosophical, 45; varieties of interpretation, 78; as in Croce and Bosanquet, 79–80; as in Ruskin, 80; romantic version, 80; distinguished from material and formal value, 113n109; of utility, 113n114; method of, 117n59; mentioned, 24, 83, 87, 113n111

Fechner, Gustav Theodor, 26, 99–100
Feeling: derivation and location, 7; and value, 8; of space, 16; and imagination, 28; of the poet, 46; and poetry, 47; and painting, 73; and intuition, 84; and vital harmony, 87; of form, 88; imagined, 102; objectified, 108n14; of relation, 111n69; aesthetic, 113n105; immediate, 113n107; mentioned, 6, 11, 50, 85–86, 89, 98, 119n118
Fichte, Johann Gottlieb, 116n51
Fine Art: distinguished from art, 58–60, 69, 124n100; and the Life of Reason, 59, 64; and utility, 61, 122n57; and sense, 67; analogy to nature, 73; distinct from beauty, 81; and automatism, 122n57; and industry, 123n63; and progress, 123n64, 124n92; and reason, 124n97; and moral function, 124n98; and illusion, 125n123; and life, 125n121; and passions, 125n106; mentioned, viii–ix, 1, 64–66, 71, 74, 78, 87, 102, 123n65, 124n105, 115n113,117,120. See also Art
Fine artist, 74–77
Form: and material, 14–15; province of, 14; and optical physiology, 15, 17; as perception of a synthesis, 15; as extension, 16; elements of, 16, 24, 111n63; from multiplicity in uniformity, 16; varieties of, 16–17, 19–20; assigned to an indeterminate object, 17–19, 112n84; as multiplicity in uniformity, and defects of, 17; and pleasure, 19; given as determinate, 19–20; abstract, 20–21, 24; and utility, 20; fitness of as expression, 22–23; and essence, 87; intuition of, 88; and aesthetic value, 100, 112n90; effect of, 110n48; classification of, 111n67; appercep-